# The Savvy Guide to the 4-Year WUE COLLEGES

# The Savvy Guide to the 4-Year WUE Colleges

By Brian Swan

Published by Greatland College Consulting
5015 E 98th Avenue
Anchorage, AK 99507
www.greatlandcollegeconsulting.com

Copyright 2016, 2017, 2019, 2024, 2025 by Greatland College Consulting

All rights reserved. No part of this book may be reproduced or transmitted in any from or by any means, electronic, mechanical, photocopying, recording or otherwise, without the written permission of Greatland College Consulting except where permitted by law.

Written by Brian Swan
Illustrated by Bob Parsons
WUE Guy design by Alex Parsons
Edited by John Meyer, Cape Fear Publishers
Cover design by Kathleen Meyer, Cape Fear Publishers
Layout by John Meyer, Cape Fear Publishers

Trademarks: All brand names, product names and services used in this book are trademarks, registered trademark or tradenames of their respective holders. Greatland College Consulting is not associated with any college, university, product or vendor.

Disclaimers: The author and publisher have used their best efforts in preparing this book. It is intended to provide helpful and informative material on the subject matter. Greatland College Consulting makes no representations or warranties with respect to the accuracy or completeness of the contents of the book. Greatland College Consulting specifically disclaims any responsibility of any liability, loss or risk which is incurred as a consequence, directly or indirectly, of the use and application of any of the contents of this book.

WUE (r) and WICHE (r) are registered trademarks owned by the Western Interstate Commission for Higher Education, which was not involved in the production of this product nor has in any way endorsed this product.

Fifth edition. ISBN: 978-0-9977735-5-2

Please send comments and corrections to:
brianswan@greatlandcollegeconsulting.com

# The Savvy Guide to the 4-Year WUE COLLEGES

### Brian Swan

How to save on tuition at 94 colleges
and universities in 16 western states through
the Western Undergraduate Exchange programs.

Fifth edition, 2025

# About the author

Brian Swan is an Independent Educational Consultant and founder of Greatland College Consulting. He is a member of the Higher Education Consultants Association and the Seattle Area College Counselors. He is passionate about helping students find the right college fit.

He lives with his wife and dog in Anchorage, Alaska, where he takes full advantage of the city's urban amenities, as well as the nearby recreational opportunities in this biggest and wildest of the western states.

# Table of contents

**Preface** .................................................. page 1

**The WUE Guy** ........................................ page 30

**The colleges**

    Alaska ............................................. page 33

    Arizona ............................................ page 41

    California ......................................... page 49

    Colorado .......................................... page 59

    Hawaii ............................................. page 81

    Idaho .............................................. page 87

    Montana ........................................... page 97

    Nevada ........................................... page 113

    New Mexico ..................................... page 121

    North Dakota .................................... page 135

    Oregon ........................................... page 149

    South Dakota ................................... page 163

    Utah .............................................. page 177

    Washington ..................................... page 191

    Wyoming ........................................ page 203

**The lists** ............................................. page 207

**Acknowledgements** ............................. page 246

**Alphabetical index** .............................. page 248

The Savvy Guide to the 4-Year WUE Colleges

# Preface

The idea for this book began at the University of Alaska College and Career Fair a few years ago. I noticed that the tables with banners from colleges that read "WUE" were some of the most crowded. I began to look into the WUE or Western Undergraduate Exchange programs offered through WICHE, the Western Interstate Commission for Higher Education. Are you already getting confused?

I then began to browse through the requirements to get accepted into the various colleges that offered the discounted WUE tuition rate. That's when I noticed a wide range in how they determined who would be eligible for the reduced tuition. Test scores, high school curriculum, and the competitive nature of the WUE programs were different for each state and each school. What applicants needed to know about those differences went above and beyond just getting accepted into a particular college and taking the necessary steps to receive the WUE tuition discount. I spent a lot of time flipping back and forth from page to page, website to website, to make sense of it all. The WUE website, while decent, was just a starting point. I decided I would make a database for myself to make all this information organized and comparable. Although there are more two-year WUE colleges than four-year, most of the students and families I work with were interested in the four year schools.

Then someone suggested that I publish the data I had gathered, as many students, parents, and counselors would love to have this information. And thus it was born: *The Savvy Guide to the 4-Year WUE Colleges*. This endeavor did not take great deal of skill. Most people could get this data for themselves. It just took time. A lot of time.

Hopefully I'll save you hours of searching and exploring. I tried to be as accurate as possible with the information I collected. Any errors are my own and I would love to correct them if you find any. You can email me at brianswan@greatlandcollegeconsulting.com if you believe I mis-stated something.

## What is WICHE?

This definition adapted from information supplied by wiche.org

"WICHE (Western Interstate Commission for Higher Education) is a regional, nonprofit organization. Membership includes the 16 western states/U.S. Territories (CNMI and Guam). WICHE and its 16 member states work to improve access to higher education and ensure student success. Our student exchange programs, regional initiatives, and our research and policy work allow us to assist constituents throughout the West and beyond.

"WICHE is the only organization in the West that focuses exclusively on higher education issues, from access and accountability to tuition and fees to distance learning and innovation, providing hard data on the trends as well as analysis. In the West, public higher education is the primary backbone of the economy, and WICHE's policy research and collaborative programs work toward the goal of supporting the West's citizens and its constantly evolving cultures."

*Under WICHE's Western Undergraduate Exchange, students pay 150 percent of the receiving school's resident tuition, substantially less than standard nonresident tuition. Some 40,000 students enrolled in 2023-24, saving an average of $11,000 each in tuition, or some $556 million total.*

What this means is basically this. Instead of every state providing every educational opportunity, the fifteen western states have combined to share many of their programs with each other's residents. These types of collaborations exist in other geographically similar areas of the United States.

## What is WUE?

An updated version of information from wiche.org: "WUE (pronounced "woo-wee") is the Western Undergraduate Exchange, and it is coordinated by WICHE. WUE is a regional tuition-reciprocity agreement that enables students from WICHE states to enroll in more than 150 participating two- and four-year public institutions at 150 percent of the enrolling institution's

# Preface

resident tuition. WUE is the largest program of its kind in the nation, and has been in operation since 1987! WUE is not a short-term exchange—it is meant to be used for a full degree."

This book is focused only on the WUE program. To be eligible for WUE, students must be a resident of one of the WICHE states, which are:

- Alaska
- Arizona
- California
- Colorado
- Hawaii
- Idaho
- Montana
- Nevada
- New Mexico
- North Dakota
- Oregon
- South Dakota
- Utah
- Washington
- Wyoming
- Guam and the Commonwealth of the Northern Mariana Islands

The formula, in theory, is quite simple. Say you live in California and want to see what the tuition would be to attend a hypothetical public WUE school in Colorado. We'll call this school Colorado U. It has an in-state tuition of $10,000 and an out-of-state tuition of $25,000. In this scenario:

The in-state tuition at Colorado U . .$10,000
    times 1.5 (150 percent) . . . . . . . . . . .$10,000 x 1.5 = $15,000
The WUE tuition is . . . . . . . . . . . . . .$15,000

If you lived in a non-WUE state, you would pay out-of-state tuition: $25,000.

WUE tuition . . . . . . . . . . . . . . . . . . . . .$15,000
Regular out-of-state tuition . . . . . . . . .$25,000
You save each year . . . . . . . . . . . . . . . .$10,000

Tuition does not count fees such as activity fees, maintenance fees, registrar fees, etc. These fees are mandatory and are added after the tuition. WUE doesn't account for room and board either, nor books. So fees, books, and room and board are added apart from the WUE tuition.

| | |
|---|---|
| In-state tuition | $10,000 |
| plus room and board | +$10,000 |
| plus fees | +$1,000 |
| plus books | +$1,000 |
| In-state costs | $22,000 |
| WUE tuition | $15,000 |
| plus room and board | +$10,000 |
| plus fees | +$1,000 |
| plus books | +$1,000 |
| WUE costs | $27,000 |

So that's how WUE works . . . in theory. Because of the complexities of funding and determining tuition for public universities, it gets more complicated. Many schools state their WUE tuition as an award that is *subtracted* from out-of-state tuition costs. Some call it an award and some consider it a scholarship. In addition, if you look at many schools and multiply their published in-state tuition by 1.5, you'll get a different tuition figure than what's stated on the WUE pages elsewhere on their websites! The way mandatory fees are factored into the stated WUE tuition varies from institution to institution. Most admission counselors—and myself—can't figure out all the complexities that lead to these numbers.

*But what's important is that you will save a lot of money by receiving the benefit of the WUE tuition rate.*

The bottom line is that this guidebook uses the tuition figures and fees using the latest data I could find for tuition figuresand fees from each college's website for their WUE- eligible students. They are as accurate as I can get them to be.

Wiche.edu has a great FAQ section but, in fact, many of the answers to

# Preface

those frequently asked questions state that you have find out more from the various colleges. The WUE website goes a good job of showing some of the information about the colleges, but many other factors are not addressed on the website and they are very important. *That is the purpose of this guide.* This is a one-stop shopping guide, if you will, to beginning the process of researching the colleges and universities that participate in the WUE program. One note I would add is that some of the "flagship" universities for each state do not participate. Those include The University of Colorado (Boulder), The University of Washington, The University of California schools (except Merced), and The University of Oregon. On the other hand, WUE is offered at many public two-year or community colleges across the west. I have chosen to make this a guidebook only for the four-year schools, as I have found that most students are looking to go away to the same school for four years, if at all possible. Private schools are not part of the WUE program. Only public schools. WUE tuition is only for full-time students and cannot be used for online programs and classes.

## How to use this book

This is a guidebook. It aims to help guide you in the process of looking for the best college for you. The figures I use are the following:

Under "current students"
- The number of full-time undergraduate students
- The number and percentage of WUE students
- The percentage of freshmen from out of state
- The percentage of freshmen living in on-campus housing
- The percentage of all students living in on-campus housing
- What percentage of freshmen return for their sophomore year
- The institution's four-year and six-year graduation rate

Under "admissions"
- The percentage of freshman applicants that are accepted
- The median range of standardized test scores (SAT / ACT) of admitted freshmen

- Grade point average

Under "cost"
- Tuition for WUE students
- Average room and board for on-campus housing
- Mandatory fees
- Other costs to attend college
- Approximate total cost to attend a particular college

One thing to remember, and this is important: the data supplied tell only part of each college's story. Numbers do not really tell us the quality of teaching. Data does not tell us the spirit of a university. Metrics do not tell us how intense a discussion might be in a typical political science class or the passion of a professor of medieval history. They can give us a sense of some aspects of a particular college and that is why I include them in this book.

# Preface

For the most part, this is not an opinion book. I do not give any ratings. I will try to guide the reader into how to interpret the data I have collected. And the most important thing to remember is not where you go to school, but what you do when you're there. Do you seek out the best teachers or the easiest graders? Do you pick a class because it will be interesting and will enhance your critical thinking skills or because it fits in your schedule? Do you join a club so it will look good on your resume or because you want to explore something new? None of your answers to those questions would be incorrect. It depends on what you want to get out of your college experience.

The data I chose to use can be useful in finding the school that best fits what you're looking for in your college experience. If tuition is your biggest concern, focus on the low-cost schools. If you want a larger or smaller WUE school, make sure you focus on that part. If you want to be with several others who are also from out of state, take a close look at that metric. In other words, decide what's important to you and use this book as a guide to help you find your best college fit.

## How not to use this book.

Small statistical differences do not matter. A college that has 8 percent of students from out of state is not much different, as far as that particular data point is concerned, than a school that has 12 percent of students from out of state. On the other hand, a school that accepts 100 percent of its applicants is different from a school that accepts only 60 percent of students who apply. A school that has 65 percent of its freshmen return for their sophomore year is not necessarily better than a school that has 58 percent of its freshmen return. There may be many reasons for the difference. It is important that you decide for yourself the importance of each piece of data. The data I chose are based on my experience in what most students are looking for when they go to college. Use the book as a guide, not a scorecard.

## How each college is set up

When I'm working with students on their college choices, I use the following sixteen characteristics as part of the college search:

The Savvy Guide to the 4-Year WUE Colleges

This guidebook will help with these seven characteristics:
1) Size—The number of full-time undergraduate students (not part-time), and not the number of acres that make up the size of the campus, although they are related.
2) Location—state, downtown, suburb, rural, very rural
3) Cost—a lot, or a real lot.
4) Selectivity—how many students who apply get accepted
5) Academic environment – the guide will touch on this
6) Student life—the guide will touch on this
7) Brand name importance—do you want to go to a school people you know have heard of?

You will have to explore these seven characteristics on your own
8) *Your major—The WUE website does a good job with this*
9) Student body characteristics—the kind and variety of students that attend the college
10) Student life—what do most students do while not in class?
11) Weekend environment—what do most students do on weekends?
12) Political environment—left, right, to what degree and how visible
13) Core requirements—how many and the scope of classes that are required to graduate with a degree
14) Your activities—can you pursue your nonacademic passions at that school?

The last two characteristics that I use do not apply to any of the WUE schools.
15) Religious—none is religious
16) Single sex/ethnicity—none is single sex or has a historically ethnic foundation

Here is the standard template I use.

## Name of college or university

City, state, (that city's population) and what major city it is near.
Website

# Preface

**Overview** of the school

**WUE requirements and procedures** for acceptance as a student and to receive the WUE tuition rate. Often a combination of Grade Point Average (GPA) and standardized test scores, either the ACT or SAT.

**Deadline** for applying and being eligible for the WUE tuition

**Required/recommended high school coursework**

**Information about current students**

Number of full time undergraduates

The number and percentage of WUE students

Percentage of freshmen from out of state

Percentage of freshmen in on-campus housing

Percentage of all students in on-campus housing

Percentage of freshmen returning for sophomore year (freshman retention rate)

Percentage of freshmen who will graduate in four years (Four-year graduation rate)

Percentage of freshmen who will graduate in six years (six-year graduation rate)

**Admissions statistics**

Percentage of freshman applicants offered admission (freshman acceptance rate)

ACT median score range

SAT median range

**WUE costs**

WUE tuition

Average room and board

Mandatory fees

Approximate total cost of attendance (COA)

**Majors eligible** for the WUE tuition. Not all majors are always available for WUE students

**Getting to campus via air travel**

**Transfer information**

**Contact information**

**Insights from the admissions office**

**Insights from others**

Let's look at a fictional university that I'll call Brian U. Here's what the template looks like:

Preface

## Brian University
Eagle River, AK (pop. 7,000) about ten miles north of Anchorage
www.brianu.edu

## Overview
This picturesque campus located right in the mountains is perfect for the student who wants to learn in the cold. All the classes are outdoors. We strive to help students who can survive in both an intense academic environment and very cold weather. Our professors keep things warm with lively discussions and many hands-on experiences.

## WUE requirements and procedures
GPA of 3.0 and ACT score of 21 or SAT combined score of 1,000.
Fill out the WUE application form prior to enrollment.
Deadline March 31

## Required/recommended high school coursework

English: .......... four years
Math: ............ three years (Algebra I, Geometry, Algebra II)
Science: .......... two years (one year must include a lab)
Social studies: ..... three years
Foreign language: .. one year

## Current students

Number full time undergraduate students: ...... 5,000
Number of WUE students/percentage: ...... 250/5%
Percentage of freshmen from out of state: ........ .20%
Percentage of freshmen in on-campus housing: .... .60%
Percentage of all students in on-campus housing: ... .20%
Percentage freshman retention: ............. .75%
Four-year graduation rate: ............... .35%
Six-year graduation rate: ................ .50%

## Admissions

Acceptance rate: .......... .75%
ACT median range: ....... 21-26
SAT verbal median range: .. 500-600
SAT math median range: .. 500-600

## WUE costs

WUE tuition: ......... $10,000
Average room and board: ..$10,000
Mandatory Fees: ......... $2,000
Other: .............. $4,000
Total cost of attendance: ...$25,000

## Eligible majors

All majors are eligible for WUE except for Outdoor Studies

### Insights from admissions

*This is a made-up college. Please don't waste your time looking at this college.*

### Insights from others

*Brian thinks he's funny, but he should stick to helping students find the right college fit.*
    *Brian's wife, Jessica*

## Air travel information

From the Anchorage Airport (ANC) shuttles run during peak times. Taxis are around $40.

## Transfer information

Transfers are eligible for WUE as long as they have a GPA of 3.0 and no more than 64 transferrable credits.

## Contact information

brianswan@greatlandcollegeconsulting.com

# Interpreting each metric

## Location

Location is often important to students. Distance from home is a consideration for almost every student. For WUE students, distances will be longer, since all the options are for out-of-state schools and the thirteen western states in the contiguous United States. Of course, Hawaii and Alaska have their own distance issues. For WUE students, distance matters because of the obvious: getting yourself and all your stuff to and from campus every year. The time and cost factor to return home for school breaks or personal reasons is something to consider. As is the ease by which parents or family can visit you. These are important factors and part of every decision.

Students also need to consider how close to a major city they want to live. Campuses can be in the heart of downtown in a major city, such as The University of Colorado at Denver. They may be very far from any major city, such as University of Montana Western. Distance and access to all of a city's amenities may be important to students. Some students don't care at all. The size of the city a campus is near may also be important. The population and amenities of the largest city near your campus can affect your college experience. Some people are fine with a city that has four restaurants, a movie theater, and a grocery store. Others want access to a Broadway production or major orchestra. I've included the population of the city that the campus is located in and how far away it is from the nearest "major" city. I'll let each student decide what a major city is. It could range from Seattle, Washington to Des Moines, Iowa. Another factor is the setting of the campus. Is it within a city? Is it downtown or in a residential part of the town? Is the campus "out in the middle of nowhere"? Eastern New Mexico University is in Portales, New Mexico. Portales is around one hundred miles from Amarillo and Lubbock, Texas and more than twice that distance from Albuquerque. These campuses will all have a different "vibe." Washington State University is in Pullman, Washington. I think it would be fair to say that Pullman is a college town. A walk or bus ride will take you to many amenities that college students desire, but is not a major metropolitan location. Why is this important? Weekend activities, air travel, or just getting off campus have importance to all college students. How much will vary according to your personal preference.

**Bottom line: How far away from home is a major consideration, both financially and practically. Also, living in a major city, residential neighborhood, or a more rural setting might be a factor to consider.**

## WUE requirements and procedures

Many schools will give you the WUE tuition rate when you are accepted. Some will give you the rate after acceptance *and* after you fill out a form showing that you are WUE eligible. Sometimes that requires proof of residency in a WUE state. Some colleges set higher standards to receive the WUE rate. You might meet the criteria for acceptance, but not to receive the WUE tuition rate. Lastly, some schools are very limited and competitive in awarding the WUE tuition rate to just a few select students out of those who apply. Make sure you know how each school awards the WUE. Hopefully this guide will be very helpful in that regard.

## Deadline

Most schools have deadlines for you to get your application to them or you won't be admitted. Usually these are firm deadlines, but not always. Some colleges consider WUE a scholarship and have a scholarship deadline

# Preface

that is *earlier* than the regular acceptance deadline. Make sure you know the deadline for acceptance *and* to get the WUE tuition rate!

## Understanding high school requirements or recommendations of each state

WUE schools are all public schools. Because of that, some schools have *required* high school classes for admittance that reflect their state's guidelines for high school graduates (see California, for example). Many individual states will have specific course requirements to graduate from high school. These same requirements are needed for admittance into that state's public colleges. That makes sense. Most states require the following:

- Four years of English
- Three years of math (usually algebra, geometry, and algebra II)
- Two years of science
- Two years of social studies
- Two years of the same foreign language
- One year of arts or another class

Let's break these down a little.

English: Some states just require four years of "English." Some are more specific by requiring literature and writing. Film studies may count as an "English credit" in your state, but not in the state where the WUE school is located.

Math: Some WUE schools require four years of math: algebra I, geometry, algebra II, and a fourth math course beyond algebra II.

Science: Some WUE state schools require one or two years. Others further specify by having requirements of a certain amount of lab sciences. That is, astronomy or zoology would be a science, but not a lab science. Some will specify biology, chemistry and physics as the required lab classes.

Social studies: Some states will specify American history or world history as a requirement.

Foreign language: Most require one or two years of the same language. They will also use the term "world language." American Sign Language usually qualifies.

Performing or visual arts: Some states require a semester or a full year of studying an art or participating in a performing art such as band, orchestra, theater, or choir.

Other requirements: Some states require another class from the above categories, like an additional year of science or social studies, or a class like computer science or another college preparatory class that doesn't fit the main five areas of study.

**Bottom line: Although many of the WUE school websites say the high school curriculum listed is *"required,"* it does not always mean that if you are missing one or two of the requirements you won't get accepted. I would think of the term more like *"strongly recommended."* In most cases, admissions will look at out-of-state students a little differently in regard to required courses.**

If you are considering a WUE option, it would be helpful to look at the state requirements at the beginning of each state section to see how your curriculum compares to some of the WUE schools in the states you might be looking at. If necessary, you could make some junior or senior year adjustments to your class choices.

You're very safe if you take the following:
- English: Four years of college prep English.
- Math: algebra I, geometry, algebra II, and a fourth year of math.
- Science: biology, chemistry, and physics.
- Social studies: two years, including American and world history
- Foreign language: two years of the same language
- Art: one year

Of course, the more you challenge yourself, especially in the areas you are interested in, the better a candidate you'll be at any college. My advice would be to be careful to take enough classes in the areas where you aren't as strong. Because the WUE schools reflect their states' requirements for their college-bound high school students, they have only a certain amount of flexibility in these requirements.

# Current Students

## Number of full time undergraduates

The number of undergraduate students I use is the number of full time undergraduate students. Since almost all students attending an out of state college are full time, this number seems the most useful. Many campuses, especially in larger cities, have a lot of part time students and those students often take classes in the evenings. This is a very different type of student than the "normal" full-time, attending-during-the-day type of student. Some colleges have 1,000 full-time students and 1,000 part-time students. For an out-of-state student, those 1,000 part-time evening students would have very little interaction with the full-time students. They also tend to be less engaged with the extracurricular activities such as music and sports than the rest of the student body. Because of those factors, the number of undergraduates listed in the guide is full-time students. I also did not include graduate students as they tend to be older and more professionally oriented students who are often in just one building. The casual interactions between undergraduates and graduate students are usually not a significant part of the undergraduate experience. So the number of undergraduate students I use is the number of full-time undergraduate students.

## Number and Percentage of WUE students

At some colleges, WUE is very popular and at others it is almost non-existent. This variation is due to many factors. The largest factor, in my opinion, is that the colleges that have the smallest number of WUE students tend to be colleges that focus on serving students in their local area. Many of these students also commute to school and tend to be less involved in campus events.

Most students attending an out-of-state college want to be with students who are also involved in the total college experience. Including the number of students attending the college and receiving the WUE tuition rate, I think, shows how popular the WUE is at that college. A large number or percentage of students who are getting the WUE tells me that the process is not difficult and that the college wants to attract out-of-state students with the WUE tuition waver. This information, along with the percentage of out-of-state students, is helpful in the decision-making process. A college with a large percentage of WUE students would be a more attractive option for most families. A college with a very small number of WUE students would be a red flag. It doesn't mean that the school is a bad choice or a bad college, but I think there is a reason why that college doesn't have a lot of WUE students. Just knowing that information will help you make a wiser decision in your college choice.

## Percentage of freshmen from out of state

All WUE students are, by definition, out-of-state students. All campuses have out-of-state students, but the number or percentage can vary immensely. Many WUE schools have fewer than 2 percent of their students from out of state. This does not make them better or worse, but from my experience, it does give the student body and campus a different feel. Now for many western states, an in-state student may live very far from campus. They may be from a large city, small town, or a farming community. But generally, the higher percentage of in-state students means that they live "nearby." They may be a diverse group of students, but not geographically diverse. They can more easily go home for a weekend. They know the city and the area pretty well. Out-of-state students find going home or visiting friends is much more difficult in comparison. They also don't know the area as well. Where to go for a day hike? The best place to see a show? While figuring out these things can be fun and part of the college experience, it is different when you are two out of a hundred from out of state. It's just a different vibe. The transportation to and from campus is usually more "on your own" at a school with fewer out-of-state students. A school with 20 to 30 percent of its students from out of state will have more geographic diversity. You may meet people from all over the United States. How important is this? Each student is different and each can decide how important that factor is. I have included it in the guidebook because I think it is something that should be considered.

Bottom line: Would you prefer to be one of the few out-of-state students or be in a school with a larger population from outside the state?

Preface

## Percentage of freshmen in on-campus housing and percentage of all students in on-campus housing

Living on campus is a different dynamic than commuting to campus. It's not necessarily better or worse, but is an important factor to many students. Students at colleges change and mature a lot during their time. Freshmen, more often than not, are living on their own for the first time and making more and more decisions on their own. Seniors are past that point in their lives and are looking for full-time jobs, comfortable on their own, and eager to take the next step. For most colleges, a majority of freshmen live on campus; this is sometimes required. As they progress, more and more students live off campus or in campus apartments. For out-of-state students, where and how you will live while away at college is a bigger consideration than for students who live nearby. Unless you have relatives or close friends you'll be living with and commuting to school, housing is an important consideration. Some colleges consider the residential component essential to the college experience at their institutions. Others don't. For most WUE students, this factor is something to consider.

While this guidebook does not get into each school's specific housing and dining options, the percentage of students who are in on-campus housing is included for a few reasons. The greater the percentage, the greater the housing options usually are. This just makes sense. Also, the greater the percentage, the greater a sense of a residential community exists. Commuters can be very involved in campus activities and those who live in dorms might be less involved, but as a general rule, those who live on campus are more involved in campus activities. As an out-of-state student, WUE students will be with more students like themselves (meaning from out of state) at schools that have a larger percentage of students from out of state. As with all the other metrics, the quality of your college experience will not be determined solely by whether or not you live on campus, but it is an important consideration. So I think the percentage of freshmen that live in on-campus housing is something that should be considered. (Note: Some universities have smaller "satellite" campuses that usually don't have campus-provided housing options. These are designed primarily for students in those cities and the surrounding areas and I have not included them in my data.)

**Bottom line: As an out-of-state student, how important would it be to you to have a significant portion of your peers also living in dorms, especially the first couple of years?**

## Percentage freshman retention

The freshman retention rate is what percentage of freshmen return for their second or sophomore year. One might think that the higher the rate, the better the school, but I think it tells more about the type of student and about the students' willingness to return. Let me explain. If you look at the schools with the highest freshman retention rates, it usually mirrors the schools with the lowest acceptance rates. Why? Well, those who get accepted into a "top" university are the type of students who are likely to return for their sophomore year. If you took the same pool of students and they went to other schools as freshmen, they would be highly likely to return to those schools as well. Some schools with lower retention rates have freshmen who might be "seeing if college is for them."

Some other reasons for lower rates are financial. Students may take off after their freshman year to earn more income. They may also decide that college is not for them. They may have been marginal students who didn't really want to go to college, but thought it was "the thing to do." They might have discovered that the school they chose was not the right fit for them. They might start at a local or lower-cost school and then transfer to the school they prefer after having a year under their belt to figure out what they really want to major in.

As you can see, there are many reasons freshmen do not return for their second year. The freshman retention rate tells more about the types of students and their situations than the quality of the education offered. Having said that, I have found that most students want to go to a school where most of the students—and the friends they make—will be back for their second year. That's why I included the freshman retention rate and why it can be a useful tool to help you consider the school you want to go to.

**Bottom line: How important is it to you to know that most of the freshmen who start out at your college return for their sophomore year?**

## Four-year and six-year graduation rates

Four-year and six-year graduation rates tell us what percentage of students graduate in four years and what percentage of students graduate in six years. This is the least reliable data I've included. How to arrive at these numbers can be complicated. If a student transfers because they've decided to switch majors and their current school doesn't have their desired major, does this count as a student who didn't graduate in four years or six years? A student who stays out of college for a year to earn money and then returns: how is

this calculated in the percentage? One would think that the higher the rate, the better the school, but like the freshman retention rate, this piece of data tells us more about the students in general than the school's ability to help their students graduate in four years. Ideally, most students would like to go to school full time for four years and get a degree. Statistically, less than one fourth of college students complete their degree in four years.

In my opinion, the four-year residential college experience is more of a "Hollywoodized" version of college. It often takes more than four years because of the students' various situations. It's usually not the failure of the college to graduate their students in four years. Many of the reasons why students don't return for their second year are also reasons why students don't graduate in four years. Attending part time, switching majors, taking a year off are the most common reasons. Others are transferring schools or changing your mind about what you want in your college experience. As far as college is concerned, it is not unusual for eighteen- or nineteen-year-olds to figure out what they want out of their college experience as they go. How many adults are still figuring out "what to do?" Most students who graduate in four years have a pretty clear plan and the resources—money—to so. So, like the freshman retention rate, this tells us more about the students who attend the college than about the college itself.

The schools with the highest four-year and six-year graduation rates have the types of students who are usually high achieving and driven and have

# Preface

the resources to graduate in four or six years. A school with a very low four-year graduation rate has a lot more students who are attending part time or taking a class or two to see if college is for them, and students taking longer for financial reasons. None of these factors reflect on the quality of education. I still find it a useful tool, though, because it does say something about the students. Like the freshman retention rate, it might be a one of the factors for WUE students to consider.

**Bottom line: How important is it to you to journey together as a class of freshmen and to graduate in four years?**

## Freshman acceptance rates

One of the sad things in college admissions today is the race to see which schools can admit the lowest percentage of students who apply. Lately Harvard and Stanford have been neck and neck in turning away over 95 percent of the very qualified applicants they receive each year. Many students and families think that if there is so much demand for a particular school that they have to turn so many away, it must be a "good" school. The *U.S. News and World Report* rankings and the schools themselves have helped fuel this demand. As the percentages of accepted students get lower, the thought is that the quality of the students gets higher. There's a lot of debate about this in general that I will not discuss here, but the data is useful information for WUE

school applicants. All but four colleges accept over half the students that apply. Most accept two-thirds to three-fourths of applicants. Many accept over 90 percent and some accept 100 percent. These are open enrollment colleges and they will enroll anybody. Students will be enrolled in the appropriate classes as determined by the college. Yes, there is college for everyone. I have included the data so students and families will have an idea of their chances of acceptance, not as a tool to see which of the schools is better.

**Bottom line: Use the acceptance rate to help gauge your chances of acceptance.**

## Median SAT/ACT scores

Standardized testing has been around for a long time. It is a flawed system and has many detractors. WUE schools use standardized test scores a lot because of their efficiency. Nobody has come up with a better, *more cost effective,* system to date. Since each state's taxpayers provide most of the funding for their public universities and colleges, so cost effectiveness is a very important factor. The use of a student's grade point average (GPA) and standardized test scores creates the easiest way to determine each applicant's quality. How well students test, how hard they work, and special family and school situations do not show up very well in these figures. Students and families that know how the system works are at a much greater advantage than those applicants who don't—who are often those with lower incomes or are the first in their family to attend college. But be that as it may, using standardized test scores and GPA it's the most cost effective way to measure students' qualifications. (Along with the classes they take, as I discuss below). This edition uses the SAT Math and Critical Reading scores that range from 200 to 1,600. I do not include the writing score. I use the traditional ACT scores from 1 to 36 without the writing. Some states, like California or Colorado, use a grid to come up with a single number that represents a combination of GPA and test scores. For each of the standardized tests, I have included the median 50 percent range of students admitted. This means that 25 percent of the students scored higher and 25 percent scored lower than the range. For example, an ACT median of 20 to 24 means than half of the students accepted at that college had ACT scores in this range, 25 percent were higher, and 25 percent were lower. Once you receive your test scores, it can be helpful to see if you are in the range of most of the students who are accepted. If you are above the range, you will probably be accepted (assuming you took the required high school curriculum). If you are within the range, you have a good chance to be accepted. If you are below the range, your chances are less. Colleges will also look at GPA and the classes you took. But standardized test scores, for better or worse, are a helpful tool to predetermine what your chances of acceptance at a certain school might be.

Bottom line: While most colleges are still test optional, meaning you aren't required to submit a standardized test score, submitting your test score may help your admission chances. Knowing the test scores of other students who have applied to a college you are interested in gives you an idea of whether that particular college is a good academic match for you.

## Average GPA

The average high school GPA (Grade Point Average) of students applying to a particular college. This gives you an idea of what your chances of offer of admission are and how your GPA compares to others applying to a particular college. With more schools being test optional, this has taken on a bit more importance.

## WUE cost of attendance

Cost of attendance for this guidebook is broken down into four sections:
1) WUE tuition
2) Average room and board for on-campus housing
3) Mandatory fees
4) Other costs

By adding these four figures together, families can get an idea of what the total college costs are for each WUE school.

## WUE tuition

While it might be said that tuition is 150 percent of the in-state rate, it can get little more complicated than that. WUE is offered only to full time students. Online and part-time students are not eligible for the WUE tuition. Most colleges consider full time students to be those taking at least twelve credits per semester. Most full-time students actually take fifteen or sixteen credits, depending on the institution. Some schools charge per credit, while other have a flat rate for "full-time" students. For comparison between schools, I used sixteen credits as the standard, unless most students took fifteen. For the scope of this book, the cost difference and practical use for this variation is minimal. Some schools have out-of-state rates that are less than 150 percent of the in-state rate. In those cases, I just used the out-of-state rate.

## Mandatory fees

The tricky part comes in "fees." Some schools have just a few fees, like a $50 technology fee and a $100 student activity fee. When you add the fees to the tuition, it's just a little more. Other schools have fees that are over $1,000 each semester. Why colleges include some costs in tuition and others in fees has a lot to do with politics, funding, and things beyond the scope of this book—and my understanding. A list at the back of the book shows each school in order from lowest cost to highest cost. Other types of aid are available from all colleges. Aid based on merit or need might make the final cost of attending college less than the WUE tuition rate. And completing the FAFSA, applying early in the process, and pursuing scholarships—especially those specific to the school to which you are applying—may help you more than the WUE program.

## Average room and board for on-campus housing

Room and board is what it costs to stay on campus, in college-supplied housing, usually dorms. I use the term average because many schools have various housing and dining (board) options. Some schools have apartments or single rooms and those will cost more. Some schools will have bare-bones dining options, while others require students (especially freshmen) to buy the full meal plan of three meals a day each day of the week. At some schools you pay for what you eat, but most plans are all you can eat for each meal. Even with these variations, the average food cost is pretty much the same across the WUE schools. For this guide, I'm assuming students will eat most or all of their meals using the college dining services. Housing costs have more to do with the price of real estate where the college is located than the quality of the housing. Most students can live off campus for less than it costs to live on campus. Living on ramen noodles is a low-cost college tradition. Living with a "few" roommates off campus also can lower your costs. For most freshmen, that is a lot of responsibility added to your first year

# Preface

living away from home. For that reason, most freshmen live on campus and move off to save money as they get older and more responsible. I've used the average room and board as a way to compare the WUE schools. Off campus housing and how you feed yourself would be too much of a variable to use in a guidebook. My advice would be to use average room and board for your freshman year, knowing that it could be less (Yay!) in future years if you move off campus. On most colleges at which many students live off campus, they do not need a car to get to campus. Most students can walk or take public transportation if they choose to live off campus.

Note: Some schools* have no on-campus housing, I have used an average room and board of $9,000 to come up with their costs. Figuring lower cost for room and board off campus would be offset by increased transportation costs, maybe having a car and its costs (fuel, insurance, parking, depreciation).

(*Several WUE schools have no on-campus housing: Metropolitan State University of Denver, Nevada State University, Northern Arizona – Yuma, Northern New Mexico, Utah Valley University, )

## Other costs

This was the most difficult to compare because it varies so much between students. Other costs of attendance are most commonly books and fees. Books required for classwork can range from a few hundred dollars per year to over a thousand dollars. Additional fees above the cost of tuition can range from a few hundred to a few thousand dollars per year. I have listed the mandatory fees separately from tuition, but because these are mandatory, every student will pay most of the fees. The government requires schools to include these costs in the figures they publish on their websites so students and families have a good idea of the total cost of going to college. However, there is no standard about how to calculate these costs. The types of classes each student takes and what each professor at each school requires their students to purchase for their particular class varies immensely, making comparisons difficult.

The last major factor in the wide range of other costs, especially for WUE students, is the cost of transportation to and from school each year. Some students must fly to go to a WUE school (definitely true in Alaska and Hawaii), while others may need to drive just fifty or a hundred miles. Still others may drive several hundred miles in the fall to bring all their stuff to school, but fly back for winter or spring breaks. How often students return home is also a large cost variable.

The last variable that is hard to compare is just each student's standard of living: cell phone plans, clothing, eating out, entertainment, toiletries, and everyday living expenses are all quite variable, too. Some students spend hardly anything on these costs, while others spend significantly more. So because these variables make it hard to compare schools, I've done two things. First, I have that compares the cost of schools considering just tuition and room and board. Secondly, to get an idea of the actual cost to go to school for WUE students, I've used the same dollar amount ($4,000) to democratize all these variables. Think of "other costs" as a big pot with books, transportation to and from school, everyday and weekend living expenses all in one expensive dish. So all the school costs will have tuition plus room and board plus $4,000 and mandatory fees to give each WUE student an idea of what the total cost of attendance might be. This is different from what is on each school's website, but in a guidebook, I thought this was the best way to compare the schools and give an accurate idea of the costs for WUE students. Transportation costs are the largest variable in comparing the actual cost to attend a particular college and in what the known costs are. Families can refine their actual cost of attendance once they whittle their list down to the schools they're really interested in.

**Bottom line:** For most students and families, the cost of higher education is a huge factor. Use the WUE tuition, room and board, and total cost of attendance as a known price. Compare it to your in-state colleges and community colleges. Since you often don't know your final tuition costs from both private and public colleges until spring of your senior year, after they've determined how much aid to give you, you can have a good idea of at least these costs and compare them to the final financial aid offers you receive from all the schools you applied to.

## Getting your scholarship

The most important thing is to *apply before the school's deadline.* Some schools have WUE and scholarship deadlines that come before their final deadline for acceptance. The best advice is *to apply early!* Many schools have deadlines before November 30 of your senior year. Don't leave money on the table by missing deadlines. As far as other paperwork is concerned, most schools fall under two types: those that require paperwork to receive the WUE rate and those that don't. Those that require paperwork are simple and you just sign a paper stating you live in a WUE eligible state. You might need to provide a driver's license number or some other ID showing you live in the state, but most forms just require your address. Some schools will automatically give the rate to students from the WUE states with no additional paperwork. It's important to know which schools require additional steps; that information is included in this guidebook.

## Keeping your scholarship

Most schools require you to be full time and have a minimal grade-point average. If your school requires paperwork for the WUE, it usually has to be filled out each year. You may not change your status to become an in-state student after you have attended and lived in the state for a year or two. Once you accept the WUE, you are an out of state student for the entirety of your time at that college.

The Savvy Guide to the 4-Year WUE Colleges

# Meet The WUE Guy!

To help guide on you the road to choosing your college, I'd like to introduce you to The WUE Guy. He's here to give you a quick glance at who most likely will qualify for the WUE tuition rate. The WUE Guy will be holding one of three road signs:

If the WUE Guy is holding a **"GO"** sign, it means that WUE is automatically awarded to students who are offered admission and they are from a WUE state. So if you meet the admission requirements and are offered admission, you will get the WUE tuition rate. It also means all majors are available to WUE students.

OR

Some colleges require a minimum GPA of 2.0 or 2.5 to receive the WUE tuition rate.

If the WUE Guy is holding a **"B"** sign, it means that students who are offered admission and wish to receive the WUE tuition rate are required to have a higher GPA and/or test scores than other admitted students. These are often B or B+/A- students and/or usually all the majors are available for WUE students.

If the WUE Guy is holding a **"Caution"** sign, it means to be careful when thinking about receiving the WUE tuition rate at these schools because of one or more of the following:

The WUE scholarship is a competitive one and only some students receive it, so be aware only a limited number of students can expect to receive it.

OR

The WUE requirements for GPAs and test scores are significantly higher, often much higher, than needed to be offered admission and to be granted the WUE tuition rate. Make sure you are aware of what combinations of GPAs and test scores will grant you an admission offer AND the WUE tuition rate.

OR

WUE is available to only a few majors

So caution does not mean to not apply, it just means to research thoroughly and be aware of how that college awards the WUE tuition rate.

# Alaska

The University of Alaska, Anchorage is the state's largest and is largely a commuter school. It is an open enrollment institution. The University of Alaska Fairbanks focuses more on arctic research and engineering. The University of Alaska Southeast is the smallest and is the closest to a traditional liberal arts college.

# WUE Colleges in
# alaska

# University of Alaska Anchorage

Anchorage, AK (pop. 295,570)
www.uaa.alaska.edu

## Overview

Surrounded by an environment both urban and wild, the **University of Alaska Anchorage** is the state's largest university, at the heart of its largest city. UAA faculty and students live and work in the nation's only arctic state and seek to leverage Alaska's position as the "gateway to the Arctic" to broaden understanding of arctic issues among citizens, policymakers and colleagues at all levels. UAA students have received many prestigious national and international scholarships and awards including Fulbright, Truman, Rhodes, Marshall, Gates Millennium and more.

## Current students

Full time undergraduates . 4,351
WUE students . . . . . 141/3%
Freshmen out of state . . . . 7%
Freshmen in housing . . . . NR
All students in housing . . . NR
Freshman retention . . . . . 69%
Four-year graduation rate. . 22%
Six-year graduation rate. . . 32%

## Deadline

All the paperwork must be turned in by the add/drop class deadline.

## Admissions

Acceptance rate . . . . . . . 82%
ACT median range . . . . 17-25
SAT median range. . 1020-1260
Grade-point average. . . . . NR

## WUE costs

WUE tuition . . . . . . . $11,584
Average R & B. . . . . . $14,744
Mandatory fees . . . . . $1,594
Other . . . . . . . . . . . $4,000
COA . . . . . . . . . . . $31,922

## WUE requirements and procedures

WUE is automatically awarded upon admission.

# Alaska

## Required/recommended high school coursework
None is actually required; open enrollment into associate's degree program and then can progress into a bachelor's degree program.

## Eligible majors
All majors are open to WUE students.

## Air travel information
Anchorage Airport has taxis/Uber/Lyft for around $40 and public buses also run to the campus.

## Transfer information
2.8 GPA and all programs are WUE eligible.

## Contact information
admissions@alaska.uaa.edu

### Insights from Others
*Although largely a commuter school, its location in Anchorage is wonderful for those who want a somewhat large city surrounded by the great Alaskan outdoors. Lots of different classes and times are available. Those who live on campus are a pretty tight-knit group. Also, it's a good school for engineers.*
*Brian Swan*
*Greatland College Consulting*
*Anchorage, AK*

The Savvy Guide to the 4-Year WUE Colleges

# University of Alaska Fairbanks

Fairbanks, AK (pop. 99,357)
www.uaf.edu

## Overview

At the **University of Alaska Fairbanks** we don't just offer degree programs; we offer life-changing experiences and boundless opportunity. Engineer and build bridges. Learn to speak Yup'ik. Launch a rocket. Monitor muskoxen. You'll venture outside the classroom, where fieldwork really is in the field—unless it's in the forest, ocean, or any of the rugged terrain that makes up Alaska's vast, natural laboratory. Around here, if you're game, you're in.

## Current students

Full time undergraduates . 2,276
WUE students . . . . . .231/10%
Freshmen out of state . . . .18%
Freshmen in housing . . . .56%
All students in housing . . .36%
Freshman retention . . . . .72%
Four-year graduation rate. .13%
Six-year graduation rate. . .33%

## Admissions

Acceptance rate . . . . . . .70%
ACT median range . . . . 18-25
SAT median range. . 1085-1280
Grade-point averge . . . . .3.46

## WUE costs

WUE tuition . . . . . . .$15,660
Average R & B. . . . . .$13,220
Mandatory fees . . . . . . . .$0
Other . . . . . . . . . . . $4,000
COA . . . . . . . . . . .$32,880

### Insights from admissions

*UAF is a traditional college campus with an active and engaged student body, and endless opportunities for exploration, recreation, and self-discovery. We are situated in Alaska's beautiful interior, and are ranked as one of the country's top colleges for outdoor activities. We also have small class sizes and an 11:1 student to faculty ratio, and we have an emphasis in hands-on learning and undergraduate research opportunities. Come check us out! www.uaf.edu/admissions/visit*

# Alaska

## Deadline
June 15

## WUE requirements and procedures
WUE is automatically awarded upon admission.

## Required/recommended high school coursework
- English . . . . . . 4 years
- Math . . . . . . 3-4 years (algebra I, geometry, algebra II, trigonometry, elementary functions, pre-calculus, calculus)
- Social studies . . 3-4 years
- Science . . . . . 3-4 years (includes 1 lab in biology, chemistry, physics)
- Foreign language . 2 years

## Eligible majors
All majors are open to WUE-eligible students.

## Air travel information
Taxi/Uber/Lyft for around $20 or bus for around $2 from the airport to campus.

## Transfer information
Transfer students are eligible for WUE after completing the WUE application.

## Contact information
admissions@uaf.edu
www.uaf.edu/admissions/visit

## Insights from others
*UAF is a research university in a truly near-arctic setting. It's a great school for anything related to arctic issues. Fairbanks is a pretty small town and, yes, it can get below zero for a few weeks at a time. But don't worry, you'll survive the winters. It's also a good school for engineers, those interested in the oil industry, and climate change effects.*

*Brian Swan*
*Greatland College Consulting*
*Anchorage, AK*

# University of Alaska Southeast

Juneau, AK (pop. 32,556)
www.uas.alaska.edu

## Overview

The **University of Alaska Southeast** is located in the temperate **rain forest** of Alaska. It's also situated **right on the ocean** and in the capital city of Juneau. UAS takes advantages of its location in it's offerings to students.

## Current students

| | |
|---|---|
| Full time undergraduates | 484 |
| WUE students | 58/12% |
| Freshmen out of state | 8% |
| Freshmen in housing | 20% |
| All students in housing | 10% |
| Freshman retention | 63% |
| Four-year graduation rate | 13% |
| Six-year graduation rate | 32% |

## Admissions

| | |
|---|---|
| Acceptance rate | 63% |
| ACT median range | NR |
| SAT median range | NR |
| Grade-point average | NR |

## WUE costs

| | |
|---|---|
| WUE tuition | $11,584 |
| Average R & B | $13,454 |
| Mandatory fees | $1,920 |
| Other | $4,000 |
| COA | $30,958 |

### Insights from admissions

*We also offer the "Come Home to Alaska" program where students with a lineal ancestor (parent, grandparent, etc.) who is an Alaska resident can receive resident tuition regardless of residency.*

### Insights from others

*This hidden gem is a small school at a public school price. If you're interested in living in a temperate rain forest right on the ocean, and in some great dorms, look at UAS. Marine science is especially strong here.*
  Brian Swan
  Greatland College Consulting
  Anchorage, AK

# Alaska

## Deadline
August 1

## WUE requirements and procedures
WUE is automatically awarded upon admission after completing the WUE tuition request form.

## Required/recommended high school coursework

- English . . . . . . 4 years
- Math . . . . . . . 4 years
- Social studies . . . 4 years
- Science . . . . . . 4 years

OR

- English . . . . . . 4 years
- Math . . . . . . . 3 years
- Social Studies . . . 4 years
- Science . . . . . . . years
- Foreign language . 2 years

## Eligible majors
All majors are open to WUE-eligible students.

## Air travel information
If the student lets Student Housing know of their arrival date/time, **the housing office can pick them up.**

## Transfer information
If more than 30 credits, must have a 2.0 GPA. If less than 30 credits, must meet same requirements as freshmen: 3.0 GPA OR 2.5 AND ACT 18/SAT 1290

## Contact information
admissions@uas.alaska.edu

Arizona State University is actually three campuses, all in Tempe, that are connected via shuttle. Students enroll at ASU and can live near or attend any of the campuses. It is by far the largest WUE college in Arizona. Northern Arizona University is a medium to large sized WUE school in Flagstaff. The University of Arizona in Tucson has only two majors eligible for the WUE so is not included. As well as the University of Arizona – Sierra Vista campus has only 4 majors eligible. Very few students use the WUE at these colleges, so they are not included. The University of Arizona is listed as a WUE school, but offers only one major to WUE students.

# WUE Colleges in
# arizona

The Savvy Guide to the 4-Year WUE Colleges

## Arizona State University

Tempe, AZ (pop. 166,842) near Phoenix
(includes Downtown, Polytechnic and West campuses)
www.asu.edu

### Overview

**Arizona State University (ASU)** is creating a new model for American higher education, an unprecedented combination of academic excellence, entrepreneurial energy and broad access. This New American University is a single, unified institution comprising four differentiated campuses positively impacting the economic, social, cultural and environmental health of the communities it serves. Its research is inspired by real world application, blurring the boundaries that traditionally separate academic disciplines. ASU serves more than 80,000 students in metropolitan Phoenix, Arizona, the nation's fifth largest city. ASU champions intellectual and cultural diversity, and welcomes students from all fifty states and more than one hundred nations across the globe.

### Current students

Full time undergraduates  59,832
WUE students . . . . . 792 / 1%
Freshmen out of state . . . . .38%
Freshmen in housing . . . .71%
All students in housing . . .24%
Freshman retention . . . . .85%
Four-year graduation rate. . .41%
Six-year graduation rate. . .68%

### Admissions

Acceptance rate . . . . . . .90%
ACT median range . . . . 19-27
SAT median range. . 1120-1370
Grade-point average. . . . .3.55

### Insights from admissions

*WUE is a great option for students who would otherwise not receive a merit-based scholarship and are interested in one of the majors offered through the program. The overall savings amount to roughly $10,000, while our merit-based scholarships range from $8 to 14,000 a year. While these awards cannot be combined with WUE, any scholarship above $10,000 will be a better value. Calculate your estimated merit-based scholarship at this site:*
*scholarships.asu.edu/estimator*

42

# Arizona

## WUE costs
WUE tuition . . . . . . . $17,733
Average R & B. . . . . . $17,754
Mandatory fees . . . . . *$,753
Other . . . . . . . . . . . $4,000
COA . . . . . . . . . . . $41,827
*ranges from $1,153 to $2,393

## Deadline
You must be admitted and enrolled by the time classes start. Give at least 6-8 weeks for decisions to be generated.

## WUE requirements
First year students must meet one of the following: 3.0 GPA in core courses, SAT of 1180 or ACT of 24. First year students are required to live in ASU residence halls during their first year.

## Required coursework
See complete list in Appendix A on page 46.

## Eligible majors
Check ASU's website WUE page for the list of about 100 eligible majors.

## Air travel information
Phoenix airport has light rail connections directly to campus.

## Transfer information
Transfers with a GPA of 2.5 are eligible for WUE.

## Contact information
asurecruitment@asu.edu

### Insights from others
*For a large state university, ASU does its best to make its students not just a number. Unlike its peers, classes don't fill up and spaces are available. The Barrett Honors College requires a separate application and is worth looking into at this beautiful campus.*
    *Evelyn Jerome-Alexander*
    *Magellan College*
    *Counseling*
    *Topanga, CA*

The Savvy Guide to the 4-Year WUE Colleges

# Northern Arizona University

(includes Yuma campus)
Flagstaff, AZ (pop. 67,468)
www.nau.edu

## Overview

**Northern Arizona University,** located in Flagstaff, Arizona, is a Public High-Research Activity University, offering ninety-one undergraduate degree programs. NAU is located on the Colorado Plateau at 7,000 feet, has a four-season climate and is two hours north of Phoenix. To ensure your future success, we are committed to placing the needs of you, the learner, at the center of everything we do. Our distinguished professors are committed not only to teaching you, but serving as mentors and working with you as well. Here, hands-on learning and the opportunities for research and creative pursuits are available to you!

## Current students

Full time undergraduates  20,010
WUE students . . . . 4641/23%
Freshmen out of state . . . .27%
Freshmen in housing . . . .83%
All students in housing . . .41%
Freshman retention . . . . .76%
Four-year graduation rate. . .43%
Six-year graduation rate. . .59%

## Deadline

July 1.

## Admissions

Acceptance rate . . . . . . .82%
ACT median range . . . . 19-25
SAT median range. . 1060-1260
Grade-point average. . . . . 3.7

## WUE Costs

WUE tuition . . . . . . .$18,144
Average R & B. . . . . .$14,432
Mandatory fees . . . . . $1,344
Other . . . . . . . . . . . $4,000
COA . . . . . . . . . . . .$31,920

## WUE requirements and procedures

WUE is automatically awarded upon admission

## Required/recommended high school coursework

See complete list in Appendix B on page 47.

# Arizona

## Eligible majors
All majors are eligible to WUE-eligible students

## Air travel information
The most cost-effective way is to fly to Phoenix and rent a car for a one-way trip to Flagstaff. Flagstaff does have a regional airport with flights to and from Phoenix.

## Transfer information
WUE is awarded upon transferring.

## Contact information
admissions@nau.edu
nau.edu/admissions/financing/western-undergraduate-exchange/

### Insights from admissions
*At Northern Arizona University, you'll find opportunity in every direction. Experience a different Arizona at 7,000 feet and with four distinct seasons, all in one of the nation's top-ranked college towns. With nearly 100 bachelor's degrees, award-winning study abroad programs, and countless opportunities for unique undergraduate research and experiential learning opportunities, you can truly go anywhere from here.*

### Insights from others
*Although NAU is the third largest public school in Arizona, it is significantly different from its gigantic ASU and UA sister schools. Flagstaff is a small, quaint town that has a much more mountain feel than desert. It snows often in the winter! Notable programs include education, communications and a very reputable hospitality program. I like to recommend the Honors program for my strong academic students as well!*
   *Erin Mitchell*
   *Educational Consultant*

## APPENDIX A

## Required/recommended high school coursework
## Arizona State University

- English . . . . . . . . . . 4 years (composition/literature based)
- Math . . . . . . . . . . . 4 years (algebra I, geometry, algebra II and one course requiring algebra II as a prerequisite)
- Laboratory Science . . . 3 years total (1 year each from any of the following areas are accepted: biology, chemistry, earth science, integrated sciences and physics)
- Social Science. . . . . . . 2 years (including 1 year American history)
- Second Language. . . . . 2 years (same language)
- Fine Arts or Career and Technical Education . . 1 year

## APPENDIX B

## Required high school coursework, Northern Arizona University

- English . . . . . . 4 years (composition/literature based) or ACT 21 English SAT verbal
- Math . . . . . . . 4 years algebra 1, geometry, algebra 2 and an advanced math for which algebra 2 is a prerequisite
- Social studies 1 years American history (or 560 on SAT subject test) and one year of European history, world history, economics, sociology, geography, government, psychology or anthropology, or SAT subject test score of 580 on world history
- Science . . . . . . 3 years biology, chemistry, earth science, or physics. An integrated science class may be substituted for one required course. Or two years of one of the above and an ACT science score of 20 or SAT subject test score of chemistry 600, biology 590 or physics 620
- Foreign language . 2 years or AP 3, Clep 50, IB 4, or SAT 50th percentile
- Fine Art. . . . . . .1 year or career and technical education

California is the most complicated system to navigate of all the states involved in WUE. It has the most schools, with fifteen being part of the WUE program. But not many students take advantage of the California WUE colleges. Many of the colleges are commuter schools, where most of the students commute to school and the colleges are really designed to serve the students in the surrounding area. Only two (Cal Poly Maritime and Cal Poly Humboldt) have more than 3 percent of their freshmen enroll from out of state. I've NOT included the following WUE colleges because they have less than 1 percent of their students

CONTINUED ON NEXT PAGE

# WUE Colleges in california

taking advantage of the WUE tuition rate AND no more than 60 total students who attending who are WUE students, which averages about one quarter of one percent at each of these following colleges:

CSU – Bakersfield

CSU – Channel Islands

CSU – Chico

CSU – Dominguez Hills

CSU – East Bay

CSU – Monterey Bay

CSU – Northridge

CSU – San Bernardino

CSU – San Marcos

CSU – Stanislaus

U Cal – Merced

Again, these are all WUE colleges, but very few students actually take advantage of the WUE program so I felt a detailed review was not needed for this edition of the guidebook.

All this information is found at the CSU Mentor website. If you're considering a WUE school in California, go to CSUmentor.edu!

## Complication number 1:

California has a strict application period. You may apply as a freshman only from October 1 to November 30 of each year. No exceptions.

## Complication number 2:

California's university system also has very strict high school course requirements. Unlike many other states, California's high school course requirements are not negotiable. If you are short a class, you will not be admitted. You must have at least a C or better in each class. Below are their requirements:

English (four years of college preparatory English composition and literature) four years

Math (four recommended, including Algebra I, Geometry, Algebra II, or higher) three years

Science (including one biological science and one physical science) two years

Social Studies (one year of US history or one semester of US history and one semester of civics or American government AND one year of social science)

Foreign Language (two years of the same language or ASL, unless you are bilingual) two years

Visual and performing arts (dance, drama or theater, music, or visual art) one year

College preparatory elective (additional year chosen from the University of California list) one year

Must have these 15 required courses.

You can visit any of the colleges' website or CSU Mentor for more details.

## Complication number 3

"Impaction" is the term the colleges in California use when too many students are applying for a limited number of spots. If this is the case, California students who live near the specific colleges will get preference in admission. After the "local admission area" students have applied and accepted admission, then students outside the area are offered enrollment based on their eligibility index. The higher your index, the more likely you'll get accepted. Impaction may also involve certain majors in high demand. Some campuses have no impaction, while others have several majors that are impacted. Nursing is almost always impacted and therefore not available to out-of-state students. How impaction affects each college and each major changes every year.

Bottom line: applying to the colleges in California is very complicated. If you are thinking about any of the schools, go to csumentor.edu and be well informed about all the aspects of applying. Those include classes taken, the correct way to calculate your GPA for California colleges, calculating your eligibility index and any effects that impaction may have on your choice.

# Cal Poly Maritime Academy

Vellejo, CA (pop. 120,000) thirty miles from San Francisco
www.csum.edu

## Overview

Cal Poly Maritime enrolls nearly 1,000 students and offers specialized programs to prepare them for careers in engineering, international business, logistics, international relations, global trade, marine transportation, oceanography, and related fields. **Cal Poly Maritime's** degree programs include practical applications, with every student participating in labs, simulators, an international study experience (via our Training Ship *Golden Bear* or land-based international experience), and industry internships.

## Insights from admissions

*A key part of the campus experience is the annual training cruise aboard our 500-foot training ship "Golden Bear." She serves as a floating classroom/laboratory where classroom concepts in marine transportation, engineering and technology are practiced and applied. School-sponsored, study-abroad trips provide those studying international business, logistics, maritime security and maritime policy with a first-hand exposure to those practices in locations around the world.*

## Current students

Full time undergraduates . . 911
WUE students . . . . . 118/13%
Freshmen out of state . . . . 16%
Freshmen in housing . . . . 93%
All students in housing . . . 77%
Freshman retention . . . . . 78%
Four-year graduation rate. . 58%
Six-year graduation rate. . . 68%

## Deadline

November 30.

## Admissions

Acceptance rate . . . . . . . 76%
ACT median range . . . . 21-26
SAT median range. . 1070-1260
Grade-point average. . . . . 3.43

## WUE Costs

WUE tuition . . . . . . . $9,675
Average R & B. . . . . . $15,160
Mandatory fees . . . . . $2,213
Other . . . . . . . . . . . $4,000
COA . . . . . . . . . . . $31,048

California

## Required high school coursework
- English . . . . . . 4 years
- Math . . . . . . . 4 years   algebra, geometry, advanced algebra
- Social studies . . . 2 years   1 year US history or 1 semester of civics or American government AND 1 year of social science
- Science . . . . . . 2 years   1 biological and 1 physical
- Foreign language . 2 years
- Fine Art . . . . . . 1 year .
- Elective . . . . . . 1 year   from the above categories

## WUE requirements and procedures
WUE is awarded upon admission.

## Eligible majors
All majors are open to WUE-eligible students.

## Air travel information
No reasonable public transportation is available to get to campus from the nearby airports. Contact the school for more information or assistance.

## Transfer information
Must have a 2.5 GPA.

## Contact information
admissions@csueastbay.edu

### Insights from others
*Students at Cal Poly Maritime are members of the Corps of Cadets, wearing uniforms to class and for all campus responsibilities (including meals and on-campus jobs), and are required to "fall in" three times weekly for a roll-call activity. Cal Poly Maritime students are extremely focused on their future careers, and the university is focused on helping students find jobs and they succeed, with 94 percent of graduates finding jobs within six months of graduation. Cal Poly Maritime has about 85 percent male and 15 percent female students.*

*Evelyn Jerome-Alexander*
*Magellan College Counseling*
*Topanga, CA*

## Cal Poly Humboldt

Arcata, CA (pop. 17,726)
275 miles north of San Francisco
www.humboldt.edu

### Overview

Cal Poly Humboldt emphasizes hands-on undergraduate research and intensive faculty mentoring of students. Humboldt has long been a place where students come to discover their futures, chart their paths, and become the innovators of tomorrow. You'll be part of a campus known for its longstanding commitment to social and environmental responsibility. Now, as **Cal Poly Humboldt,** that responsibility has more weight than ever — and we're excited to rise to the challenge. Field research often supplements classroom and academic pursuits are melded with the unique terrain and climates of the Pacific Northwest.

### Current students

Full time undergraduates . 4,717
WUE students . . . . . 201/4%
Freshmen out of state . . . . 7%
Freshmen in housing . . . .86%
All students in housing . . .38%
Freshman retention . . . . .76%
Four-year graduation rate. .28%
Six-year graduation rate. . .47%

### Deadline

November 30

### Admissions

Acceptance rate . . . . . . .83%
ACT median range . . . . 21-28
SAT median range. . 1030-1280
Grade-point average. . . . . 3.5

### WUE Costs

WUE tuition . . . . . . .$11,980
Average R & B. . . . . .$14,306
Mandatory fees . . . . . . . .$0
Other . . . . . . . . . . . $4,000
COA . . . . . . . . . . .$30,286

### WUE requirements and procedures

Must have a minimum GPA of 3.0 in listed secondary school units ("a-g") required to be eligible.

# California

## Required high school coursework
- English . . . . . . 4 years
- Math . . . . . . . 4 years  algebra, geometry, advanced algebra
- Social studies . . . 2 years  1 year US history or 1 semester of civics or American government AND 1 year of social science
- Science . . . . . . 2 years  biological and 1 physical
- Foreign language . 2 years
- Fine Art . . . . . . 1 year
- Elective . . . . . . 1 year  from the above categories

## Eligible majors
All majors are open to WUE-eligible students.

## Air travel information
The Arcata-Eureka airport is about a ten-minute drive from campus. It is served by United Airlines and offers rental cars.

## Transfer information
If you have 60 transferable semester credits or less, you must have a GPA of 2.0.

## Contact information
hsuinfo@humboldt.edu

## Insights from others
*Cal Poly Humboldt is a great residential college with a small population, making class size and professor accessibility much greater than at your larger CSU schools. It has a very Pacific Northwest feel, from the huge forests to the gray skies and cold water. This is an old logging town, not a beach town. Students tend to be liberal and accepting. It has more of an outdoors, environmental vibe; in a nutshell, way more flannel, a lot less tie-dye. Strong programs for Humboldt are environmental sciences and the arts, though there are many majors to choose from.*
*Erin Mitchell*
*Educational Consultant*
*San Diego, CA*

# Cal Poly Pomona

Pomona, CA (pop. 149,058)
www.cpp.edu

## Overview

Striking a balance between urban excitement and rural charm, **Cal Poly Pomona** is nestled in 1,438 rolling acres on the eastern edge of Los Angeles County. Due to its location at the nexus of Los Angeles, Orange and San Bernardino counties, the university's students can swim in the ocean, ski in the mountains and visit the world's happiest amusement park the same day. **Cal Poly Pomona** is known for its learn-by-doing philosophy. Our graduates are ready to succeed in the professional world on Day One.

## Current students

Full time undergraduates   21,824
WUE students . . . . . 23/<1%
Freshmen out of state . . . . 2%
Freshmen in housing . . . .44%
All students in housing . . .10%
Freshman retention . . . . .86%
Four-year graduation rate. .21%
Six-year graduation rate. . .72%

## Deadline

Must apply between October 1 and November 30.

## Admissions

Acceptance rate . . . . . . .56%
ACT median range . . . . . NR
SAT median range. . . . . . NR
Grade-point average. . . . . 3.8

## WUE Costs

WUE tuition . . . . . . . $9,675
Average R & B . . . . . .$16,770
Mandatory fees . . . . . $1,700
Other . . . . . . . . . . . $4,000
COA . . . . . . . . . . .$32,145

## WUE requirements and procedures

Award recipients are selected based on their academic profile (GPA and SAT/ACT test scores), and will be issued to the top 15% of WUE admits.

## Required high school coursework

- English . . . . . . . . . . 4 years of college preparatory English composition and literature
- Math . . . . . . . . . . 4 years (Algebra, geometry, advanced algebra)

# California

- Social Studies . . . . . . . 2 years (1 year of US history of 1 semester of us history and 1 semester of civics or American Government AND 1 year of world history, culture, and geography)
- Science . . . . . . . . . . 2 years ( 1 biological and . . . . . . 1 physical)
- Foreign Language . . . . 2 years of the same language
- Visual and performing arts art . . . . . . 1 year
- Elective . . . . . . . . . . 1 year of any college preparatory subject

## Eligible majors
All majors are available to WUE eligible students

## Air travel information
Taxi, car rental, Lyft and Uber are available from LAX, the Ontario International, and John Wayne airports.

## Transfer information
Transfers are eligible for two years of WUE

## WUE contact information
admissions@cpp.edu

### Insights from others
*Cal State Poly is Southern California's Polytechnic Institute. Besides engineering and sciences, pre-vet and architecture are strong programs. Because of impaction, when you apply list at least one non-impacted major if you want to help your chances of admission..*
*Evelyn Jerome-Alexander*
*Magellan College Counseling*
*Topanga, CA*

## APPENDIX A

### Air travel information, Cal Poly Maritime

From Oakland Airport (OAK), take BART to El Cerrito del Norte stop, then Take SolTrans route #80 bus to Vallejo Transit Center and the route #3 bus to the Cal Poly Maritime Campus.

From San Francisco Airport (SFO), take BART to Embarcadero stop and walk two blocks to the Ferry Building. Take the Vallejo Ferry to the Vallejo Ferry Terminal/Bus Transfer Center. Take the SolTrans route #3 bus to Cal Poly Maritime's Campus.

Colorado

Colorado has ten four-year WUE colleges. The University of Colorado in Boulder is NOT one of them, nor is Colorado School of Mines. Two are in Denver, Metropolitan State and the University of Colorado – Denver. These are large schools and generally commuter schools. Colorado State is also a large university, but it has many more students living in on-campus housing. Northern Colorado, Colorado Mesa and the University of Colorado at Colorado Springs are medium to large universities. Adams Sate, Colorado State Pueblo, Western Colorado and Ft. Lewis College are smaller. CU – Anschutz Medical Campus is WUE, but offers no B.S. degrees.

# WUE Colleges in
# colorado

The Savvy Guide to the 4-Year WUE Colleges

# Adams State University

Alamosa, CO (pop. 9,562) near Pueblo
www.adams.edu

## Overview

**Adams State University** is a small, four-year public institution in Colorado's beautiful San Luis Valley. Academic programs emphasize (1) experienced and supportive faculty who focus on teaching and mentoring; (2) innovative programs that incorporate experiential learning, student research, and community outreach; and (3) modern, state-of-the art facilities with first-class technology, computer labs, and learning studios..

## Current students

Full time undergraduates . 1,055
WUE students . . . . . 173/16%
Freshmen out of state . . . . 39%
Freshmen in housing . . . . 72%
All students in housing . . . 49%
Freshman retention . . . . . 54%
Four-year graduation rate. . 26%
Six-year graduation rate. . . 33%

## Admissions

Acceptance rate . . . . . . . 99%
ACT median range . . . . 16-26
SAT median range. . . 915-1125
Grade-point average. . . . . NR

## WUE Costs

WUE tuition . . . . . . . $16,494
Average R & B. . . . . . $13,118
Mandatory fees . . . . . . . . $0
Other . . . . . . . . . . . $4,000
COA . . . . . . . . . . . $33,612

## Deadline

Adams State has rolling admissions with no hard deadline.

## WUE requirements and procedures

WUE is automatically awarded upon admission.

## Required/recommended high school coursework

- English . . . . . . 4 years
- Math . . . . . . . 4 years   algebra 1 and higher
- Social studies . . . 3 years   1 year of world or American history

# Colorado

- Science . . . . . . 3 years   2 must have labs
- Foreign language . 1 year .
- Electives . . . . . 2 years

## Eligible majors
All majors are open to WUE-eligible students.

## Air travel information
Alamosa has a local airport, but most students fly to Denver and can take a bus or regional plane to Alamosa.

## Transfer information
WUE is available to all WUE-eligible students.

## Contact information
admissions@adams.edu

### Insights from admissions
*WUE students who are interested in going to school in Colorado should know that Adams State is surrounded by the beautiful Sangre de Cristo and San Juan mountain ranges in Alamosa, Colorado, making it the perfect place to study, work, and live. In addition to WUE tuition rates, we have the most generous full-time tuition window in Colorado in which students only pay the 12-credit-hour rate for up to 20 credits.*

### Insights from others
*Adams is a serene campus that feels like home—a strong community and personalized attention. Students have a lot of school spirit, possibly because about 50 percent of students are varsity athletes—everybody knows somebody on the team.*
  *Glenda Durano*
  *College Advising and*
  *Planning Services*
  *Albuquerque, NM*

The Savvy Guide to the 4-Year WUE Colleges

# Colorado Mesa University

Grand Junction, CO (pop. 59,778)
about four hours from Denver or Salt Lake City
www.coloradomesa.edu

## Overview

In the heart of beautiful Western Colorado's Grand Junction, **Colorado Mesa University** is one of the fastest-growing universities in the country. With small class sizes and expert faculty, students at **CMU** can count on receiving personalized education and support. Classroom experiences consist of professors—not teaching assistants—who take a vested interest in student success. Featuring modern residence halls, state of the art facilities and labs and a thriving University Center that fosters a robust student-life atmosphere.

## Current students

Full time undergraduates . . 6,418
WUE students . . . . . 625/10%
Freshmen out of state . . . . 17%
Freshmen in housing . . . . 68%
All students in housing . . . 28%
Freshman retention . . . . . 76%
Four-year graduation rate . . 19%
Six-year graduation rate . . . 45%

## Deadline

May 1 is the priority deadline for getting the best aid, but there is no hard deadline for admission.

## Admissions

Acceptance rate . . . . . . . 63%
ACT median range . . . . 18-25
SAT median range. . . 930-1180
Grade-point average. . . . . NR

## WUE Costs

WUE tuition . . . . . . . $16,256
Average R & B. . . . . . $13,866
Mandatory fees . . . . . . $984
Other . . . . . . . . . . . $4,000
COA . . . . . . . . . . . $35,106

## WUE requirements and procedures

Must have a 2.5 GPA.

## Required/recommended high school coursework

- English . . . . . . 4 years
- Math . . . . . . . 4 years  algebra 1 and higher

# Colorado

- Social studies . . . 3 years  1 year of world or American history
- Science . . . . . . 3 years  2 must have labs
- Foreign language . 1 year .
- Electives . . . . . 2 years

## Eligible majors
All majors are open to WUE-eligible students.

## Air travel information
Grand Junction Regional Airport has service from United, American, and Delta airlines.

## Transfer information
GPA of 2.5 and up to 105 credits.

## Contact information
admissions@coloradomesa.edu

### Insights from admissions
*At Colorado Mesa University there is no separate application for the Western Undergraduate Exchange Program. Freshman and transfer students (13-90 semester credits only) with a permanent address from one of our participating western states and a minimum of 2.0 GPA are automatically considered for this reduced tuition program.*

### Insights from others
*CMU is one of those "just right schools." With 11,000 students, the school has all the amenities of a large school (Greek life, rec center, D2 athletics, honors program), but very personalized teaching. The school has some strong majors (criminal justice, forensics, nursing, radiology) and impressive facilities. CMU is great for the student who wants to take advantage of opportunities.*
   *Glenda Durano*
   *College Advising and Planning Services*
   *Albuquerque, NM*

The Savvy Guide to the 4-Year WUE Colleges

# Colorado State University – Pueblo

Pueblo, CO (pop. 108,249)
www.csupueblo.edu

## Overview

Colorado State University-Pueblo is nestled in a historically and culturally rich community of more than a hundred thousand people in the southern part of the state, near the foothills of the Rocky Mountains, and just a short drive to Denver and Colorado Springs. The state's geography and attractions create an exciting environment for this vibrant college campus. CSU-Pueblo's five thousand students thrive in small classes taught by world-class educators. Outside the classroom we foster an exciting, adventurous and social environment rich in culture, athletics, and all the beauty the Pikes Peak region has to offer. And with over three hundred days of sunshine a year, people here have a healthy love for the outdoors.

## Current students

Full time undergraduates . 2,589
WUE students . . . . . 166/6%
Freshmen out of state . . . . .21%
Freshmen in housing . . . .45%
All students in housing . . .18%
Freshman retention . . . . .63%
Four-year graduation rate. .21%
Six-year graduation rate. . .39%
(Tuition includes $2,000 reduction if living on campus, which is required for the first two years.)

## Admissions

Acceptance rate . . . . . . .99%
ACT median range . . . . 18-25
SAT median range. . . 940-1130
Grade-point average. . . . . 3.4

## WUE Costs

WUE tuition . . . . . . .$20,216
Average R & B. . . . . .$12,548
Mandatory fees . . . . . $2,170
Other . . . . . . . . . . . $4,000
COA . . . . . . . . . . . .$36,764

## Deadline

March 1

## Required/recommended high school coursework

- English . . . . . . 4 years
- Math . . . . . . . 4 years   algebra 1 and higher
- Social studies . . . 3 years   1 year of world or American history
- Science . . . . . . 3 years   2 must have labs

# Colorado

- Foreign language 1 year .
- Electives . . . . . 2 years

## WUE requirements
WUE is automatically awarded upon admission.

## Eligible majors
All majors are open to WUE-eligible students.

## Air travel information
Most students fly into Denver or Colorado Springs, but Pueblo does have a small airport (mostly connecting flights to Denver) that some students choose. The Pueblo airport is about twenty minutes from campus; the Colorado Springs airport about forty-five minutes, and Denver is about two hours. When initially visiting campus, many students and their parents rent a vehicle, but other ground transportation options are available. Many of our students also get rides to the airport from their friends.

## Transfer information
2.3 GPA and all majors are eligible

## Contact information
info@scupueblo.edu

## Insights from admissions
*With our automatic WUE tuition rate, CSU-Pueblo offers an affordable education. Our average class size of 21 creates a community on campus. Students have the unique opportunity to be involved not only in the classroom, but also throughout campus and the community with research, internship, and clinical experiences.*

## Insights from others
*CSU Pueblo has a bit of a commuter feel but is working to attract students by offering strong programs such as unique mechantronics / robotics; the education department gives students the opportunity to be in the classroom freshman year; and they have several 3+2 programs in business and the sciences.*
*Glenda Durano*
*College Advising and Planning Services*
*Albuquerque, NM*

65

The Savvy Guide to the 4-Year WUE Colleges

# Colorado State University

Fort Collins, CO (pop. 155,000)
one hour north of Denver
www.colostate.edu

## Overview

At **Colorado State University**, over 24,000 undergraduate students enjoy an environment of deep cooperative learning in over 70 majors across eight colleges. What we're really proud of is our commitment to each student as a whole person, not just inside the classroom. Students can take advantage of more than 500 campus clubs and organizations, and a culture of service permeates the University. Fort Collins, situated along the Front Range of the Rocky Mountains, offers students quick access to outdoor adventure and a stimulating, innovative community in which to live and learn.

## Current students

Full time undergraduates   22,499
WUE students . . . . 2,286 / 10%
Freshmen out of state . . . . 40%
Freshmen in housing . . . . 90%
All students in housing . . . 23%
Freshman retention . . . . . 86%
Four-year graduation rate. . 48%
Six-year graduation rate. . . 67%

## Deadline

February 1 for guaranteed WUE approval; will be awarded until August 1 provided funds are available. WUE funding usually runs out around August 1.

## Admissions

Acceptance rate . . . . . . . 63%
ACT median range . . . . 18-25
SAT median range. . 1080-1280
Grade-point average. . . . . 3.7

## WUE Costs

WUE tuition . . . . . . . $24,053
Average R & B. . . . . . $17,508
Mandatory fees . . . . . . . . $0
Other . . . . . . . . . . . $4,000
COA . . . . . . . . . . . $45,561

## Required/recommended high school coursework

- English . . . . . . 4 years
- Math . . . . . . . 4 years  algebra 1 and higher

# Colorado

- Social studies . . . 3 years 1 must be world civilizations or American history
- Science . . . . . . 3 years 2 must have labs
- Foreign language . 1 year . 2 preferred
- Electives . . . . . 2 years

## WUE requirements and procedures
3.2 GPA.

## Eligible majors
All majors are open to WUE-eligible students.

## Air travel information
Students typically fly to Denver (DIA). A couple of shuttles run from DIA to Fort Collins: Green Ride and Super Shuttle.

## Transfer information
GPA of 3.0.

## Contact information
admissions@colostate.edu

### Insights from others
*Colorado State is located in the very cool college town of Fort Collins. The fun "downtown" area is located right off campus and is full of restaurants and cafes and places for students to hang out, but is also a nice blend into the small town community. In general CSU is a very outdoorsy school; environmental science topics and forestry majors are big here.*
*Erin Mitchell*
*Education consultant*
*San Diego, CA*

The Savvy Guide to the 4-Year WUE Colleges

# Fort Lewis College

Durango, CO (pop. 17,557)
www.fortlewis.edu

## Overview

**Fort Lewis College** is the Southwest's crossroads of education and adventure. Our blend of small classes, dynamic academic programs, and a liberal arts perspective leads to transformative learning experiences that foster entrepreneurship, leadership, creative problem solving, and life-long learning. Our unique and beautiful mountain campus, on a mesa above historic Durango, Colorado, inspires an active and friendly community with a spirit of engagement, exploration, and intellectual curiosity.

## Current students

Full time undergraduates . 2,795
WUE students . . . . . 286/10%
Freshmen out of state . . . . 60%
Freshmen in housing . . . . 89%
All students in housing . . . 49%
Freshman retention . . . . . 63%
Four-year graduation rate . . 27%
Six-year graduation rate . . . 43%

## Deadline

May 1

## Admissions

Acceptance rate . . . . . . . 93%
ACT median range . . . . . NR
SAT median range . . . . . . NR
Grade-point average . . . . . 3.36

## WUE Costs

WUE tuition . . . . . . . $12,060
Average R & B . . . . . . $13,822
Mandatory fees . . . . . $2,164
Other . . . . . . . . . . . $4,000
COA . . . . . . . . . . . $32,460

## WUE requirements and procedures

GPA of 3.0.

## Required/recommended high school coursework

- English . . . . . . 4 years
- Math . . . . . . . 4 years algebra 1 and higher
- Social studies . . . 3 years 1 of world or American history
- Science . . . . . . 3 years 2 must have labs

# Colorado

- Foreign language . 1 year . 2 preferred
- Electives . . . . . 2 years

## Eligible majors
All majors are open to WUE-eligible students.

## Air travel information
Students can fly to the Durango airport. Taxis/Uber/Lyft are available for the ten-minute drive to campus.

## Transfer information
Minimum cumulative college-level GPA of 3.0 and 30 semester credits or more.

## Contact information
admission@fortlewis.edu

### Insights from admissions
*Students from WUE-eligible states can earn up to $6,000, $8,000 or $10,000 awards depending on their GPA and test scores. See our website for details.*

### Insights from others
*Colorado's public liberal art's college, Fort Lewis attracts students to its campus located atop a mesa overlooking Durango. It boasts a widely diverse student body, granting a tuition waiver to qualified Native Americans. A laid-back vibe that celebrates individualism resonates here. Mountain bikers from all over the country compete for a spot on its nationally ranked team.*
  *Sue Zoby*
  *Mission Admission*
  *Denver, CO*

# Metropolitan State University of Denver

Denver, CO (pop. 634,265)
www.msudenver.edu

## Overview

**Metropolitan State University of Denver** has transformed the lives of more than 100,000 people in Denver and Colorado through affordable degree programs, innovative public-private partnerships and a commitment to diversity. That's why **MSU Denver** now stands as a preeminent public urban university enrolling almost 17,000 undergraduate students. Located in the heart of downtown Denver, the campus provides students with an urban experience that's less than an hour from the Rocky Mountains. From the city to the slopes!

## Current students

Full time undergraduates . 9,294
WUE students . . . . . 138/1%
Freshmen out of state . . . . 5%
Freshmen in housing . . . . 0%
All students in housing . . . 0%
Freshman retention . . . . .63%
Four-year graduation rate. . 16%
Six-year graduation rate. . .29%

## Deadline

When classes start each year

## Admissions

Acceptance rate . . . . . . .98%
ACT median range . . . . 16-23
SAT median range. . . 920-1130
Grade-point average. . . . .2.56

## WUE Costs

WUE tuition . . . . . . .$20,696
Average R & B* . . . . .$17,658
Mandatory fees . . . . . $2,164
Other . . . . . . . . . . . $4,000
COA . . . . . . . . . . .$44,516
(*Off-campus housing)

## WUE requirements and procedures

WUE is automatically awarded upon admission.

## Required/recommended high school coursework

- English . . . . . . 4 years
- Math . . . . . . . 4 years algebra 1 and higher
- Social studies . . . 3 years 1 of world or American history

Colorado

- Science . . . . . . 3 years  2 must have labs
- Foreign language . 1 year . 2 preferred
- Electives . . . . . 2 years

## Eligible majors
All majors are open to WUE eligible students.

## Air travel information
Public transportation is available to campus from Denver airport (DIA).

## Transfer information
WUE is awarded to transfer students with at least 24 transferable credits.

## Contact information
askmetro@msudenver.edu

### Insights from others
*Metro State shares the urban Auraria campus with the University of Colorado Denver and the Community College of Denver, creating an academic hub in downtown Denver. While the university has no on-campus housing, student housing is easily accessible on foot or by shuttle or light rail. STEM studies are most popular, and an on-campus hotel allows students practical hospitality management opportunities.*
  *Sue Zoby*
  *Mission Admission*
  *Denver, CO*

# University of Colorado at Colorado Springs

Colorado Springs, CO (pop. 439,886)
www.uccs.edu

## Overview

The University of Colorado Colorado Springs has been rapidly growing and now enrolls over 11,000 students in a variety of unique and challenging academic programs at an affordable cost. We offer you a high-quality education with small class sizes, opportunities to interact with professors, and amazing new facilities to enhance your learning experience.

## Current students

Full time undergraduates . 8,249
WUE students . . . . . 389/5%
Freshmen out of state . . . . .20%
Freshmen in housing . . . .54%
All students in housing . . .16%
Freshman retention . . . . .67%
Four-year graduation rate. .31%
Six-year graduation rate. . .43%

## Admissions

Acceptance rate . . . . . . .85%
ACT median range . . . . 21-27
SAT median range. . 1030-1240
Grade-point average. . . . .3.43

## WUE Costs

WUE tuition . . . . . . .$20,478
Average R & B. . . . . .$14,500
Mandatory fees . . . . . . . .$0
Other . . . . . . . . . . . $4,000
COA . . . . . . . . . . .$38,978

## Deadline

None

## WUE requirements and procedures

WUE is awarded upon acceptance.

## Required/recommended high school coursework

- English . . . . . . 4 years including at least 2 years of composition
- Math . . . . . . . 3 years 4 years for College of Engineering and Applied Science
- Social studies . . . 2 years
- Science . . . . . . 3 years 2 years of lab science
- Electives . . . . . 2 years

Colorado

## Eligible majors
All majors but nursing are open to WUE-eligible students.

## Air travel information
Several shuttle companies go from the Denver International Airport (DIA) to Colorado Springs. One-way fare is around $49. Colorado Springs also has a regional airport.

## Transfer information
2.4 GPA.

## Contact information
go@uccs.edu

## Insights from admissions
*While nursing is not a WUE-eligible program, nursing students may be considered for the Chancellor's Award of $10,000 over four years.*

## Insights from others
*UCCS has been moving from a commuter school to one with the total college experience students are looking for. The area has three hundred sunny days a year and lots of access to hiking, biking, and climbing. Several new buildings and dorms are a plus. Colorado Springs offers several places for fun and internships.*
*Brian Swan*
*Greatland College Consulting*
*Anchorage, AK*

## University of Colorado at Denver

Denver, CO (pop. 634,265)
www.ucdenver.edu

### Overview

**CU Denver** is well known for our industry-leading internship opportunities that open doors for our students at some of Denver's best employers. Maybe you also knew why our location in the heart of downtown Denver is unique, with its urban lifestyle at your fingertips and the Rocky Mountains as your backyard playground. But **CU Denver** also boasts a very diverse student body population. With students from over sixty countries across the globe, our campus's rich multicultural tapestry is open, safe and welcoming to all students who wish to learn with purpose.

### Current students

- Full time undergraduates . 8,369
- WUE students . . . . . 441/5%
- Freshmen out of state . . . . .18%
- Freshmen in housing . . . . .30%
- All students in housing . . .19%
- Freshman retention . . . . .73%
- Four-year graduation rate. .20%
- Six-year graduation rate. . .48%

### Deadline

July 31

### Admissions

- Acceptance rate . . . . . . .72%
- ACT median range . . . . 21-28
- SAT median range. . 1040-1250
- Grade-point average. . . . .3.52

### WUE Costs

- WUE tuition . . . . . . .$24,928
- Average R & B . . . . . .$17,140
- Mandatory fees . . . . . . $790
- Other . . . . . . . . . . . $4,000
- COA . . . . . . . . . . .$46,858

### Required/recommended high school coursework

- English . . . . . . 4 years
- Math . . . . . . . 4 years algebra 1 and higher
- Social studies . . . 2 years 1 must be world or American history
- Science . . . . . . 3 years 2 must be lab based
- Foreign language . 1 year . 2 preferred
- Electives . . . . . 2 years

Colorado

## WUE requirements and procedures
WUE is automatically awarded upon admission.

## Eligible majors
All majors are open to WUE-eligible students.

## Air travel information
Denver has just built a new light rail system that runs from the airport (Denver International - DIA) to Union Station. Student would take this, called the A Line, to Union Station. From there they are about six blocks from campus and can take a cab or Uber to campus. There is NO free shuttle between the train station and campus.

## Transfer information
30 or more semester credits to be a transfer student to be considered for admission. WUE is available to transfer students.

## Contact information
admissions@ucdenver.edu

## Insights from others
*Steps from the heart of downtown Denver on the shared Auraria campus, CU Denver represents the urban college lifestyle. While most students commute on buses or by light rail, several nearby housing options are popular. In addition to its downtown location, nursing students study at the top-notch Anschutz Medical Center, just a short train ride away.*
*Sue Zoby*
*Mission Admission*
*Denver, CO*

## University of Northern Colorado

Greeley, CO (pop. 96,539)
www.unco.edu

### Overview

The **University of Northern Colorado** is Colorado's most affordable research university, offering students the opportunities and connectedness of a small college along with the nationally recognized programs, research agenda and facilities of a mid-sized public institution. Its 260-acre campus is in Greeley, Colorado, about one hour north of Denver. Outside the classroom, **UNC** students explore diverse interests through academic, social, philanthropic, political, cultural, sports and faith-based clubs and organizations. Students can enjoy the Colorado outdoors with workshops, trips and free equipment rentals through **UNC**'s Outdoor Pursuits program.

### Current students

Full time undergraduates . 5,364
WUE students . . . . . 419/8%
Freshmen out of state . . . .17%
Freshmen in housing . . . .80%
All students in housing . . .33%
Freshman retention . . . . .75%
Four-year graduation rate. .24%
Six-year graduation rate. . .52%

### Deadline

July 31

### Admissions

Acceptance rate . . . . . . .85%
ACT median range . . . . 21-28
SAT median range. . 1000-1190
Grade-point average. . . . .3.47

### WUE Costs

WUE tuition . . . . . . .$16,126
Average R & B. . . . . .$17,064
Mandatory fees . . . . . $2,996
Other . . . . . . . . . . . $4,000
COA . . . . . . . . . . . .$40,186

### Required/recommended high school coursework

- English . . . . . . 4 years
- Math . . . . . . . 4 years  algebra 1 and higher
- Social studies . . . 3 years  1 must be world or American history
- Science . . . . . . 3 years  2 must be lab based

# Colorado

- Foreign language . 1 year .
- Electives . . . . . 2 years

## WUE requirements and procedures
WUE is automatically awarded upon admission.

## Eligible majors
All majors are open to WUE-eligible students.

## Air travel information
A super shuttle option runs from the Denver airport (DIA) to campus. There is a discount code for UNC students.

## Transfer information
WUE is awarded to transfer students.

## Contact information
admissions@unco.edu

### Insights from admissions
*As a mid-size comprehensive university, UNC offers a large-college experience with a small-college feel. Many campuses emphasize faculty workloads toward teaching or research. At UNC we emphasize both. Our faculty are experts in their field and they enjoy teaching. We call this the teacher-scholar model. Discover the UNC difference.*

### Insights from others
*An hour north of Denver, UNC enjoys a distinctly small-town or rural feel and students often take a short walk into town to enjoy its emerging restaurant and arts scene. Because over one third are first-generation college students, UNC offers many strong student support services, complimented by its Faculty in Residence program. UNC's large recent dorm expansion earned it the "best dorms in Colorado" distinction. Remarkably, its musical theater program is one of the most competitive in the nation.*
      *Sue Zoby*
      *Mission Admission*
      *Denver, CO*

The Savvy Guide to the 4-Year WUE Colleges

# Western Colorado University

Gunnison, CO (pop. 5,873)
www.western.edu

## Overview

Western Colorado University offers a private-college experience at an affordable cost, deep in the heart of the Rocky Mountains. We deliver a full, four-year liberal arts curriculum on a gorgeous residential campus in Gunnison. With an average class size of just seventeen students, professors handcraft each student's education to fit their interests and prepare them for a career. And **Western** offers all of this at one of the best educational values in the state of Colorado.

## Current students

| | |
|---|---|
| Full time undergraduates | 1,579 |
| WUE students | 37/2% |
| Freshmen out of state | 28% |
| Freshmen in housing | 97% |
| All students in housing | 66% |
| Freshman retention | 76% |
| Four-year graduation rate | 34% |
| Six-year graduation rate | 47% |

## Admissions

| | |
|---|---|
| Acceptance rate | 91% |
| ACT median range | 21-28 |
| SAT median range | 1080-1270 |
| Grade-point average | 3.39 |

## WUE Costs

| | |
|---|---|
| WUE tuition | $14,686 |
| Average R & B | $11,083 |
| Mandatory fees | $4,035 |
| Other | $4,000 |
| COA | $33,804 |

## Deadline

WCU has rolling admissions with no hard deadline

## Required/recommended high school coursework

None, but HEAR requirements will help

## WUE requirements

WUE is automatically awarded upon admission.

## Eligible majors

All majors are open to WUE-eligible students.

# Colorado

## Air travel information

Gunnison Airport is five minutes from campus. Denver airport is three and a half to five hours, depending on traffic and road conditions. Montrose airport is sixty to ninety minutes from campus, and Grand Junction airport is two and a half to three hours from campus.

## Transfer information

WUE is awarded to transfer students.

## Contact information

admissions@western.edu

### Insights from admissions

*Deep in the heart of the Rocky Mountains, Western Colorado University delivers computer science, engineering, a full liberal arts curriculum and career preparation to 3,000 undergraduate and graduate students at an affordable cost. The university's tight-knit community ensures students receive personalized attention and gain real-world experience before graduation. Set in the unique Gunnison Valley, Western offers students endless opportunities for adventure and hands-on learning, both in and outside of the classrooms.*

### Insights from others

*Students here live for the outdoors and, many times, classes are held there, too. Minutes from Crested Butte, snow sports and mountain biking dominate the sports scene. The well-equipped Wilderness Pursuits program rents gear for a minimal fee so students can take full advantage of their mountain home. Western State offers generous financial aid to both in-state and out-of-state students, increasing its geographic diversity.*
  *Sue Zoby*
  *Mission Admission*
  *Denver, CO*

Hawaii

The University of Hawaii – Manoa is the largest of the state's four WUE universities and is located in its largest city, Honolulu. It's the one people think of when they say "The University of Hawaii." The University of Hawaii – Hilo is on the big island and is a medium to small university. The University of Hawaii – Maui and West Oahu are WUE, but both enroll very few WUE students so are not included.

# WUE Colleges in hawaii

# University of Hawaii – Hilo

Hilo, HI (pop. 42,263)
www.uhh.hawaii.edu

## Overview

**The University of Hawai'i at Hilo** is a public university with a comprehensive portfolio of distinguished undergraduate programs, complemented by select graduate and professional degrees. As a member of our *'Ohana* (family), we challenge you to reach your highest level of academic achievement through learning, discovery and creativity inside and outside the classroom. Our *kuleana* (responsibility) is to improve the quality of life of the people of Hawai'i, the Pacific region and the world. We are committed to excellence in higher education and learning with *aloha*. Our faculty and students undertake research activities that enhance both our students' learning and our university's contribution to academia and society. With an educational experience rooted in place, culture, and diversity, your journey is our focus.

## Current students

Full time undergraduates . 2,063
WUE students . . . . . 396/19%
Freshmen out of state . . . .31%
Freshmen in housing . . . .80%
All students in housing . . .30%
Freshman retention . . . . .70%
Four-year graduation rate. . .21%
Six-year graduation rate. . .42%

## Deadline

July 1

## WUE requirements and procedures

WUE is awarded upon admission.

## Admissions

Acceptance rate . . . . . . .80%
ACT median range . . . . 17-22
SAT median range. . . 960-1200
Grade-point average. . . . .3.36

## WUE costs

WUE tuition . . . . . . .$14,976
Average R & B. . . . . .$11,201
Mandatory fees . . . . . . $988
Other . . . . . . . . . . . $4,000
COA . . . . . . . . . . .$31,165

# Hawaii

## Required/recommended high school coursework
- English . . . . . 4 years
- Math . . . . . . 3 years  algebra 1, geometry, algebra 2
- Science . . . . . 3 years
- Electives. . . . . 7 years  college prep courses

## Eligible majors
All majors are open to WUE eligible students except nursing.

## Air travel information
Hilo airport shuttles run to campus during peak periods.

## Transfer information
Must have GPA of 2.8 and at least 24 credits.

## Contact information
uhhadm@hawaii.edu

## Insights from admissions
*The University of Hawaii-Hilo is a small to mid-sized public liberal arts and science university. Ten of the 14 world climate zones exist on the big island of Hawai'i, making it a living laboratory for the study of volcanoes, astronomy, agriculture, marine science, and other natural sciences. Connecting learning, life and Aloha, your journey is our focus at UH Hilo.*

## Insights from others
*The staff and faculty seem very caring and friendly. I sense a family-like vibe, so students feel like they have a home away from home; the true spirit of Aloha lives here. It's a small, charming campus and even though the infrastructure is older, the buildings and grounds are decorated with art and native character. Students are very involved in research and have their work published in a free student magazine available in the common areas.*

*Jackie Postelnick*
*Conscious College Planning*
*Crystal Lake, IL*

The Savvy Guide to the 4-Year WUE Colleges

# University of Hawaii – Manoa

Honolulu, HI (pop. 350,399)
www.manoa.hawaii.edu

## Overview

This is a destination of choice. Students and faculty come from across the nation and the world to take advantage of **UH Manoa**'s unique research opportunities, diverse community, nationally ranked Division I athletics program, and beautiful landscape. **UH Manoa** is consistently ranked a "best value" among US colleges and universities. Our students get a great education and have a unique multicultural global experience in a Hawaiian place of learning—truly like no place else on earth.

## Current students

Full time undergraduates 11,329
WUE students . . . . 2,262 / 29%
Freshmen out of state . . . . 46%
Freshmen in housing . . . . 48%
All students in housing . . . 20%
Freshman retention . . . . . 79%
Four-year graduation rate. . 40%
Six-year graduation rate. . . 62%

## Deadline

March 1; no separate deadline for the WUE scholarship program.

## Admissions

Acceptance rate . . . . . . . 73%
ACT median range . . . . 17-22
SAT median range. . 1080-1290
Grade-point average. . . . . 3.69

## WUE costs

WUE tuition . . . . . . . $17,280
Average R & B. . . . . . $15,216
Mandatory fees . . . . . . $882
Other . . . . . . . . . . . $4,000
COA . . . . . . . . . . . $37,378

## Required/recommended high school coursework

- English . . . . . . . . . . 4 years
- Math . . . . . . . . . . . 3 years including algebra 2 and geometry
- Social studies . . . . . . . . 3 years
- Science . . . . . . . . . . 3 years
- Other college prep . . . . . 4 years
- Electives. . . . . . . . . . 5 units

# Hawaii

## WUE requirements
WUE is automatically awarded upon admission.

## Eligible majors
All majors are open to WUE Eligible students.

## Air travel information
Shuttles ($11-18), taxi/Uber/Lyft ($30) and public bus ($3) all go to and from the airport.

## Transfer information
WUE is awarded to WUE-eligible students.

## Contact information
manoa.admissions@hawaii.edu

### Insights from others
*As one might expect, the University of Hawaii has a very laid-back feel. It also, however, has strong academics, especially in the sciences and international business. It attracts a large international population (6th most diverse) and actually offers more foreign languages (so they say) than any other school.*
**Glenda Durano**
*College Advising and Planning Services*
*Albuquerque, NM*

### Insights from admissions
*Have you ever dreamed of living and studying in Hawai'i? The University of Hawai'i at Manoa is the perfect choice for your academic journey. We provide our students opportunities to intern at marine labs working to save monk seals, at hotels training to run the front desk operations, out in the field working with engineering companies on construction projects or research opportunities working with faculty to find cures for harmful viruses. Imagine yourself making the world a better place and studying in Hawaii. We provide an unparalleled opportunity to experience one of the most unique campuses in the world. At the University of Hawai'i at Manoa, it pays to be WUE.*

Boise State is the largest of the four four-year WUE schools in Idaho. It's in the state's largest city, as well. Boise State has a helpful grid to help determine your WUE eligibility. Idaho State University and the University of Idaho are medium-sized universities. Lewis-Clark State College is the smallest and most distinctive. It's a combination community college, vocational training college, and bachelor's-degree granting college.

# WUE Colleges in idaho

## Boise State University

Boise, ID (pop. 214,237)   www.boisestate.edu

### Overview

Boise State's faculty and staff are guided by one simple but powerful conviction: our students are the future leaders, thinkers and innovators of the American West, and that future begins in the classrooms of our campus, in the heart of Boise, across the river from downtown, at the intersection of the region's centers of government, technology, business and the arts.

### Current students

Full time undergraduates   13,402
WUE students . . . . 2,542/19%
Freshmen out of state . . . . .42%
Freshmen in housing . . . .65%
All students in housing . . .18%
Freshman retention . . . . .79%
Four-year graduation rate. . .30%
Six-year graduation rate. . .60%

### Deadline

December 15; if funds are available, deadline may be extended.

### Admissions

Acceptance rate . . . . . . .84%
ACT median range . . . . . NR
SAT median range. . . . . . NR
Grade-point average. . . . . 3.6

### WUE costs

WUE tuition . . . . . . .$12,796
Average R & B. . . . . .$14,776
Mandatory fees . . . . . . . .$0
Other . . . . . . . . . . . $4,000
COA . . . . . . . . . . .$31,572

### Required/recommended high school coursework

- English . . . . . . 4 years
- Math . . . . . . . 3 years applied math 1 & 2, algebra 1 & 2, geometry, analytic geometry, calculus; at least 4 semesters must be in grades 10-12
- Social studies . . . 2.5 years
- Science . . . . . . 3 years 1 year lab
- Humanities/foreign language. . 1 year
- Fine art/other . 1.5 years speech, performing arts, additional foreign language

# Idaho

## WUE requirements and procedures
3.5 GPA; 3.9 for nursing majors.

## Eligible majors
Radiologic Science and Pre-Radiologic Science are ineligible. Nursing majors require a 3.9 cumulative unweighted high school GPA to be considered for the WUE.

## Air travel information
Boise State is three and a half miles from the Boise Airport.

## Transfer information
Must have 3.5 GPA and 26 semester credits to receive the WUE tuition.

## Contact information
bsuinfo@boisestate.edu and admissions.boisestate.edu/admissions-staff

## Insights from admissions
*For students who don't qualify for the WUE scholarship, The Summit Scholarship requires a 3.40 cumulative unweighted high school GPA and provides $10,000 in savings every year. The Ridgeline Scholarship requires a 3.20 cumulative unweighted high school GPA and provides $5,000 in savings every year. (2024)*

## Insights from others
*Boise State is known for its top-rated football program and the famous blue "smurf turf" that the team plays on. Rightly so; BSU is a college with lots of school spirit. It has all the features of a large university, but is not overwhelming in size. Students are generally enthusiastic to be there and the city of Boise offers many opportunities for internships, both in industry and state government. Lots of outdoor activities are available in the area as well.*
*Brian Swan*
*Greatland College Consulting*
*Anchorage, AK*

# Idaho State University

Pocatello, ID (pop. 53,350)
www.isu.edu

## Overview

**Idaho State University** faculty and students are leading the way in cutting-edge research and innovative solutions in the areas of energy, health professions, nuclear research, teaching, humanities, engineering, performing and visual arts, technology, biological sciences, pharmacy and business. **Idaho State University** offers exceptional academics amidst the grand natural beauty of the west. ISU is at the heart of an outdoor-lover's paradise and a short drive to some of America's greatest natural wonders and exciting outdoor recreation opportunities.

## Current students

Full time undergraduates . 5,333
WUE students . . . . . 141/3%
Freshmen out of state . . . .11%
Freshmen in housing . . . .25%
All students in housing . . .12%
Freshman retention . . . . .71%
Four-year graduation rate. . .20%
Six-year graduation rate. . .36%

## Deadline

February 15

## Admissions

Acceptance rate . . . . . . .99%
ACT median range . . . . 19-25
SAT median range. . 1240-1590
Grade-point average. . . . .3.38

## WUE costs

WUE tuition . . . . . . .$12,037
Average R & B. . . . . . $7,336
Mandatory fees . . . . . . . .$0
Other . . . . . . . . . . . $4,000
COA . . . . . . . . . . .$23,373

## WUE requirements and procedures

Preference is given to applicant with a GPA of 2.5 as well as those who meet our scholarship application deadline. Students who do not meet these criteria will be considered on an individual basis.

## Required/recommended high school coursework

None are required, but the WUE is a competitive scholarship, so following a more complete and rigorous curriculum will increase your chances of receiving the award.

## Eligible majors

All fields of study are eligible; however, some high demand or oversubscribed programs may limit the number of non-resident students who can be admitted to their programs. Check with ISU for details as this may vary year to year.

## Air travel information

Boise and its airport are about two hours away. That, and a rental car, is usually the least expensive way to get to Pocatello. You can fly to Salt Lake city and take the Salt Lake City Express bus for around $40. That's about a four-hour trip.

## Transfer information

2.5 GPA.

## Contact information

admiss@isu.edu

# Lewis-Clark State College

Lewiston, ID (pop. 32,401)
www.isu.edu

## Overview

Lewis-Clark State College (not to be confused with Lewis & Clark College in Portland, Oregon) is in Lewiston, Idaho, where two rivers (Clearwater and Snake), two cities (Lewiston and Clarkston), and two states (Idaho and Washington) come together. Founded in 1893, **Lewis-Clark State** is a public undergraduate college with a three-part mission of academic programs, professional-technical programs, and community programs. One of the top public comprehensive four-year colleges in the west, with its beautiful campus, small classes, and superb faculty, **LCSC** is often described as a public institution with the feel and quality of a private college.

## Current students

Full time undergraduates . 1,888
WUE students . . . . . 118/6%
Freshmen out of state . . . .22%
Freshmen in housing . . . .19%
All students in housing . . .10%
Freshman retention . . . . .63%
Four-year graduation rate. .22%
Six-year graduation rate. . .32%

## Admissions

Acceptance rate . . . . . . 100%
ACT median range . . . . 16-22
SAT median range. . . 880-1100
Grade-point average. . . . .3.23

## WUE costs

WUE tuition . . . . . . .$10,984
Average R & B. . . . . .$12,772
Mandatory fees . . . . . . . .$0
Other . . . . . . . . . . . $4,000
COA . . . . . . . . . . . .$27,756

## Deadline

March 1 will give you automatic consideration for the WUE scholarship. August 8 is the regular deadline.

## WUE requirements and procedures

GPA 2.5.

# Idaho

### Required/recommended high school coursework
- English . . . . . . 4 years
- Math . . . . . . . 3 years  algebra 1, geometry, algebra 2 or higher
- Social studies . . . 2.5 years
- Science . . . . . . 2 years  must have lab experience in 1
- Humanities/foreign language. . 1 year
- Fine art/other . . 1.5 years
  speech, debate, arts, additional foreign language.

### Eligible majors
All majors are open to WUE-eligible students.

### Air travel information
Lewiston, ID has an airport with service from Delta and Alaska airlines.

### Transfer information
GPA of 3.0 and at least 12 transferable credits required.

### Contact information
admissions@lcsc.edu

### Insights from others
*A unique college in that it's a smaller school, yet it combines a community college, bachelor programs and vocational training. Could be great school for a student who is not sure about vocational training or college. They could do both here. It may feel rather isolated, since there are no major cities nearby.*
*Brian Swan*
*Greatland College Consulting*
*Anchorage, AK*

The Savvy Guide to the 4-Year WUE Colleges

# University of Idaho

Moscow, ID (pop. 25,534)
www.uidaho.edu

## Overview

Since 1889, the **University of Idaho** has provided students with a transformative higher education experience that prepares them to solve real-world problems and achieve success in their lives and careers. From our beautiful residential campus in Moscow, the university's reach extends throughout Idaho. U of I is a national leader in student-centered learning and interdisciplinary research that promotes public service. We serve businesses and communities, advancing diversity, citizenship and global outreach.

## Current students

Full time undergraduates . 6,864
WUE students . . . . 1,679/24%
Freshmen out of state . . . . .30%
Freshmen in housing . . . . .86%
All students in housing . . .43%
Freshman retention . . . . .75%
Four-year graduation rate. . .34%
Six-year graduation rate. . .60%

## Deadline

February 15, although acceptance after February 15 is possible, depending on space in the programs and money available for WUE. No separate deadline for WUE scholarship.

## Admissions

Acceptance rate . . . . . . .79%
ACT median range . . . . 20-29
SAT median range. . . 950-1200
Grade-point average. . . . . 3.4

## WUE costs

WUE tuition . . . . . . .$12,914
Average R & B. . . . . .$12,136
Mandatory fees . . . . . . . .$0
Other . . . . . . . . . . . $4,000
COA . . . . . . . . . . .$29,050

## Required/recommended high school coursework

- English . . . . . . 4 years   composition, literature or language
- Math . . . . . . . 3 years   algebra 1, geometry, algebra 2, additional year strongly recommended
- Social studies . . . 2.5 years   geography, history, psychology, sociology,

# Idaho

or economics
- Science . . . . . . 3 years  anatomy, biology, chemistry, geology, earth science, physical science, physiology, physics, zoology; 1 year must be lab
- Humanities/language . . 1 year  literature, history, philosophy, foreign language, fine arts
- Fine art (see humanities, language and other)
- Other . . . . . . . 1.5 years  college preparatory: speech, debate, studio or performing arts, additional foreign language

## WUE requirements and procedures
WUE awarded upon admission.

## Eligible majors
All majors are eligible.

## Air travel information
Students who are flying in would be responsible for arranging transportation from the airport to the campus.

## Transfer information
2.5 GPA.

## Contact information
admissions@uidaho.edu

### Insights from others
U of I generally serves Idaho students and the surrounding states. It has a largest percentage of students involved in Greek life of any WUE school, but most would not describe it as a party school. Moscow is a nice college town and the area has lots of outdoor activities and attracts a lot of outdoorsy type students.
*Brian Swan*
*Greatland College Consulting*
*Anchorage, AK*

### Insights from admissions
At the University of Idaho, we're excited to participate in the Western Undergraduate Exchange program, offering students from select states the opportunity to pursue their education at a reduced tuition rate. Our campus, located in the beautiful Pacific Northwest, provides a supportive environment for academic and personal growth.

The Savvy Guide to the 4-Year WUE Colleges

# Montana

Montana has six four-year WUE schools. The largest two are Montana State University (Bozeman-MSU) and The University of Montana. They do have higher standards to receive the WUE than just admittance. Montana Tech, Montana State – Billings, Montana State Northern, and The University of Montana Western are smaller universities and all grant WUE status upon acceptance.

CONTINUED ON NEXT PAGE

## WUE Colleges in montana

Admission to any of the colleges in Montana can be determined based on any of the following Primary Requirements:
- Earn a minimum ACT composite score of 22 (20 for University of Montana Northern)
- Earn a minimum SAT total score of 1120
- Earn a minimum Cumulative GPA of 2.5
- Rank in the top half of your high school's graduating class
- Montana does require that students demonstrate readiness for college in the area of mathematics and writing. Students must meet one criterion in the following lists to demonstrate their college readiness:

## Math proficiency requirements
- A score of 22 on the ACT Math section
- or a score of 27.5 on the SAT Math Test (520 on SAT Math for tests prior to March 2016)
- or a score of 3 or higher on the AP Calculus AB or BC exam
- or completion of a Rigorous High School Core that includes four years of math with grades of C or higher
- or a score of 4 on the International Baccalaureate calculus exam

## Writing proficiency requirements
- A score of 18 on the ACT Combined English/Writing section
- or a score of 19 on the new ACT Writing Test Subscore (score of 7 on old scale of 2-12)
- or a score of 25 on the SAT Writing/Language Test (440 on SAT Writing for tests prior to March 2016)
- or a score of 7 on the SAT Essay Subscore (for tests prior to March 2016)
- or a score of 3 on the AP English Language or English Literature exam
- or a score of 50 on the CLEP Subject Exam in Composition
- or a score of 4 on the International Baccalaureate Language AI Exam

Bottom line: Students can be admitted with lower scores than the minimums. On the other hand, students can be denied admission even if they meet the minimums. These are guidelines and admission counselors also use essays, letters of recommendations, and extra-curricular activities in their determinations. However, the "requirements" are a useful tool to help students and families determine if they'll be accepted into a college in Montana.

These requirements for required high school coursework apply to all the Montana schools:

## Required/recommended high school coursework
- English ....... Four years
- Math......... Three years (including Algebra I, geometry and Algebra II. Students are encouraged to take a math course in their senior year)
- Social Studies.. Three years (which should include global studies such as world history or world geography, American history, and government, economics or Indian history)
- Science ....... Two years (one year must be earth science, biology, chemistry, or physics)
- Electives ...... Two years (foreign language (preferably 2 years), computer science, visual and performing arts, or career technical education)

# Montana State University – Billings

Billings, MT (pop. 109,059)
www.msubillings.edu

## Overview

Montana State University – Billings, Montana's "urban university," offers advantages you won't find anywhere else in Big Sky Country. Studying in Montana's largest city—the business, industry, communications and healthcare hub of the state—means you'll get a real-world education through internships in hundreds of careers. You'll get individual attention from expert professors and leave with a degree respected by leading employers and top graduate schools. Experience city life, Montana style—where it takes about an hour to go from downtown to downhill. Be ready for big sky possibilities.

## Current students

Full time undergraduates . 1,868
WUE students . . . . . 226/12%
Freshmen out of state . . . . 11%
Freshmen in housing . . . . 33%
All students in housing . . . 10%
Freshman retention . . . . . 60%
Four-year graduation rate. . 11%
Six-year graduation rate. . . 25%

## Deadline

February 1

## Admissions

Acceptance rate . . . . . . 100%
ACT median range . . . . 17-22
SAT median range. . . . . . NR
Grade-point average. . . . .3.27

## WUE costs

WUE tuition . . . . . . . $10,480
Average R & B. . . . . .$10,490
Mandatory fees . . . . . . . .$0
Other . . . . . . . . . . . $4,000
COA . . . . . . . . . . .$24,970

## WUE requirements and procedures

WUE awarded upon acceptance.

## Admission requirements and high school coursework

All Montana schools require test scores and high school courses as outlined on on "Math Proficiency Requirements" on page 98.

# Montana

However, as an open enrollment university, MSUB will admit under probation any students who are missing any requirements. This means they can enroll in classes to meet the requirements. Upon successful completion of any missing requirements, probationary status is lifted.

## Eligible majors
All majors are open to WUE-eligible students.

## Air travel information
An airport is less than a mile from campus, reachable by taxi/Uber/Lyft.

## Transfer information
GPA 2.0 and 12 or more credits eligible to apply. All majors WUE eligible.

## Contact information
admissions@msubillings.edu

### Insights from others
*Located in Montana's largest city, this pretty campus offers the small-college experience with all the outdoor activities that the state offers right outside its doors. It offers one of the few degrees in psychiatric rehabilitation that leads to becoming a licensed addiction counselor. Outdoor adventure leadership is another unique major.*
**Brian Swan**
*Greatland College Consulting*
*Anchorage, AK*

The Savvy Guide to the 4-Year WUE Colleges

# Montana State University

Bozeman, MT (pop. 39,860)
www.montana.edu

## Overview

**Montana State University** is in a class of its own. Among the top 3 percent of colleges and universities for research expenditures, undergraduates at **MSU** get research opportunities typically reserved for graduate students at other schools. **MSU**'s location at the crossroads between Yellowstone National Park and some of the biggest skiing and best rivers in America offers students a classroom, lab and playground unlike any in the world. Five mountain ranges are visible from Bozeman. Division 1 sports and a great town are all part of **MSU**.

## Current students

Full time undergraduates   12,403
WUE students . . . . 1,693 / 14%
Freshmen out of state . . . . .62%
Freshmen in housing . . . . .90%
All students in housing . . .32%
Freshman retention . . . . .75%
Four-year graduation rate. .31%
Six-year graduation rate. . .57%

## Admissions

Acceptance rate . . . . . . .73%
ACT median range . . . . 20-27
SAT median range. . 1070-1270
Grade-point average. . . . .3.64

## WUE costs

WUE tuition . . . . . . . $10,096
Average R & B. . . . . . .$14,580

### Insights from admissions

*Montana State University is designated among 130 of America's most prestigious universities with very high research activity—out of 4,338 U.S. higher education institutions—by the Carnegie Classification of Institutions of Higher Education. MSU is one of only two universities to be designated with a high undergraduate profile, meaning MSU's students have direct access to hands-on learning in the classroom and undergraduate research opportunities.*

Montana

Mandatory fees . . . . . $2,216
Other . . . . . . . . . . . $4,000
COA . . . . . . . . . . . .$30,892

## Deadline
Usually January or February.

## WUE requirements and procedures
WUE offers are limited to approximately 1,000 offers each year. For reference, there were approximately 3,300 applications for WUE for Fall 2023. The WUE Scholarship is a rigorous, competitive application due to the value of WUE. Recipients of the scholarship routinely have a cumulative 3.8+ high school GPA.

## Admission requirements and high school coursework
All Montana schools require test scores and high school courses as outlined on page 98.

## Eligible majors
All majors are open to WUE-eligible students.

## Air travel information
Shuttles run during peak season. Taxis/Uber/Lyft are available. Most students can find a ride.

## Transfer information
WUE is NOT available to transfer students.

## Contact information
admissions@montana.edu

## Insights from others
*MSU is a great college for the outdoor lover, located near skiing and Yellowstone National Park. A new state-of-the-art engineering building, popular FCS football, and more than 100 area trails are draws. They do a great job of identifying high-achieving students and helping them reach their full potential. Lots of Goldwater, Rhodes, and Gates-Cambridge scholars. WUE is competitive, but they are very generous with their other scholarships.*
*Brian Swan*
*Greatland College Consulting*
*Anchorage, AK.*

# Montana State University Northern

Havre, MT (pop. 9,771)
www.msun.edu

## Overview

Montana State University – Northern, located in north central Montana, is a four-year public university offering degree programs in agriculture, automotive, business, diesel, drafting, education, electronics, engineering, graphic design, nursing, plumbing, welding, and more. Our unique, multiple entry/exit career ladder allows students to choose programs at the certificate, associate, baccalaureate, and master's degree levels.

## Current students

Full time undergraduates . . 973
WUE students . . . . . 93/10%
Freshmen out of state . . . . .20%
Freshmen in housing . . . .39%
All students in housing . . .22%
Freshman retention . . . . .70%
Four-year graduation rate. . .24%
Six-year graduation rate. . .42%

## Admissions

Acceptance rate . . . . . . .64%
ACT median range . . . . 17-22
SAT median range. . . 770-1000
Grade-point average. . . . . 2.8

## WUE costs

WUE tuition . . . . . . .$10,270
Average R & B. . . . . . $7,840
Mandatory fees . . . . . . . .$0
Other . . . . . . . . . . . $4,000
COA . . . . . . . . . . . .$22,110

## Insights from admissions

*The Northern admissions team is available to make your application process as smooth as possible. Please give us a call or send us an email with any questions you might have. We are here to help!.*

## Deadline

The deadline to apply, get accepted and get WUE is August 29, or when school starts for the semester. It is suggested that students apply for admission much sooner, due to some limited class availability.

## WUE requirements and procedures
WUE is awarded upon admission

## Admission requirements and high school coursework
All Montana schools require test scores and high school courses as outlined on page 130, with the exception of the ACT composite score. Montana State Northern requires 20, not 22.

## Eligible majors
All majors are open to WUE-eligible students.

## Air travel information
Great Falls airport is 2 hours away by car and there are direct regional flights to Havre from the Billings airport. Amtrak also stops in Havre.

## Transfer information
GPA of 2.0 and 12 credits are eligible for the WUE in all majors.

## Contact information
admissions@msun.edu

### Insights from others
*Montana Northern has one of the few programs where a student can get a four-year degree in diesel technology, while having a typical residential college experience.*
Brian Swan
Greatland College Consulting
Anchorage, AK

The Savvy Guide to the 4-Year WUE Colleges

# Montana Tech of the University of Montana

Butte, MT (pop. 33,854)     www.mtech.edu

## Overview

**Montana Tech** offers programs of distinction. It is one of only two US schools that offer a B.S. degree in geophysical engineering; one of ten that offer a B.S. in metallurgical engineering; one of nineteen in mining engineering and one of only twenty in petroleum engineering. The student body presents a national and global snapshot with students from dozens of states and several foreign countries represented. All programs derive a special character and emphasis from the unique setting and continued tradition of high quality that has characterized Montana Tech since its founding.

## Current students

Full time undergraduates . 1,622
WUE students . . . . . 197/12%
Freshmen out of state . . . . .21%
Freshmen in housing . . . .51%
All students in housing . . .14%
Freshman retention . . . . .75%
Four-year graduation rate. .30%
Six-year graduation rate. . .57%

## Admissions

Acceptance rate . . . . . . .89%
ACT median range . . . . 19-25
SAT median range. . 1050-1320
Grade-point average. . . . .3.56

## WUE costs

WUE tuition . . . . . . .$10,076
Average R & B. . . . . .$12,120
Mandatory fees . . . . . $2,150
Other . . . . . . . . . . . $4,000
COA . . . . . . . . . . .$28,346

## Insights from admissions

*Montana Tech has repeatedly been named one of the best institutions for Return on Investment (ROI). Students who earn the WUE scholarship will pay tuition rates that often make it more affordable for them to attend Montana Tech than institutions in their own state. In addition, Montana Tech's students have opportunities to take internships right after their freshman year, which tend to pay very well. Our graduates make some of the highest average starting salaries in the nation. Maximize your ROI with a degree from Montana Tech.*

# Montana

## Deadline
January 15 for WUE (Note: this is the deadline for the scholarship application. The scholarship application is not released until the admission application is received. Students can apply through August 12, but that is not recommended.)

## WUE requirements and procedures
WUE is awarded upon admission.

## Admission requirements and high school coursework
All Montana schools require test scores and high school courses as outlined on page 98.

## Eligible majors
All majors are open to WUE-eligible students.

## Air travel information
Taxi/Uber/Lyft is available and very inexpensive. Someone from the university may be able to work with students to pick them up.

## Transfer information
GPA of 2.0 and 12 credits are eligible for the WUE in all majors.

## Contact information
enrollment@mtech.edu

### Insights from others
*Montana Tech is a true "tech" school. It's one of the few small colleges that are technical in nature with a boatload of engineering degree options, including petroleum, geophysical, and mining engineering. It is also accessible to the average student who wants to be an engineer. The school also offers a BS in nursing.*
  *Brian Swan*
  *Greatland College*
  *Consulting*
  *Anchorage, AK*

The Savvy Guide to the 4-Year WUE Colleges

# University of Montana

Missoula, MT (pop. 69,122)
www.umt.edu

## Overview

Nestled in the heart of western Montana's stunning natural landscape, the **University of Montana** is a place where top-tier students, educators and researchers from across the country and around the globe come and thrive. **UM** is in Missoula, Montana's second-largest city, with a population of eighty thousand. The university draws a diverse population to Missoula and helps cultivate an educated, engaged and vibrant community. More than thirteen thousand students attend, receiving an education in a broad range of subjects that include the trades, liberal arts, graduate and postdoctoral studies and professional training.

## Current students

Full time undergraduates . 5,781
WUE students . . . . . 841/15%
Freshmen out of state . . . . 47%
Freshmen in housing . . . . 68%
All students in housing . . . 63%
Freshman retention . . . . . 74%
Four-year graduation rate. . 23%
Six-year graduation rate. . . 47%

## Deadline

Dec. 1.

## Admissions

Acceptance rate . . . . . . . 95%
ACT median range . . . . 19-26
SAT median range. . 1110-1280
Grade-point average. . . . . 3.37

## WUE costs

WUE tuition . . . . . . . $12,976
Average R & B. . . . . . $14,566
Mandatory fees . . . . . . . . $0
Other . . . . . . . . . . . $4,000
COA . . . . . . . . . . . $31,542

## WUE requirements and procedures

WUE is Competitive and requires a 3.0 minimum GPA (weighted) A 3.9 GPA automatically qualifies for WUE.

# Montana

## Admission requirements and high school coursework
All Montana schools require test scores and high school courses as outlined on page 98.

## Eligible majors
All majors are open to WUE-eligible students.

## Air travel information
Missoula has an airport and it's a short trip to campus.

## Transfer information
3.5 GPA.

## Contact information
admiss@umontanaedu

### Insights from others
*Montana's public liberal arts college attracts students who love the outdoors. A short walk to a charming business district is a plus as well. Along with a popular sports, this makes the campus a very social and engaging place. Pre-health, biology, forestry and the honors college are strong programs.*
*Brian Swan*
*Greatland College*
*Consulting*
*Anchorage, AK*

The Savvy Guide to the 4-Year WUE Colleges

# University of Montana Western

Dillon, MT (pop. 4,201)
www.umwestern.edu

## Overview

The **University of Montana Western** is the only public university to offer Experience One, a block scheduling system where students take one course at a time. In this unique, immersive learning environment, students can maximize their potential for success. Your professors and fellow students will be your close mentors, peers and collaborators. Professors will know your name and because they only teach one class at a time, will have your full attention. As a student at **Montana Western**, you will be part of a more effective and fulfilling learning environment.

## Current students

Full time undergraduates . 1,424
WUE students . . . . . 274 / 19%
Freshmen out of state . . . . .25%
Freshmen in housing . . . .72%
All students in housing . . .33%
Freshman retention . . . . .71%
Four-year graduation rate. .45%
Six-year graduation rate. . .49%

## Deadline

July 1

## WUE requirements and procedures

Must have a GPA of 3.0 or higher.

## Admissions

Acceptance rate . . . . . . .70%
ACT median range . . . . 16-23
SAT median range. . . 870-1210
Grade-point average. . . . . 3.3

## WUE costs

WUE tuition . . . . . . . $9,877
Average R & B. . . . . .$10,525
Mandatory fees . . . . . . . .$0
Other . . . . . . . . . . . $4,000
COA . . . . . . . . . . . .$24,402

## Admission requirements and high school coursework

All Montana schools require test scores and high school courses as outlined on page 98.

# Montana

## Eligible majors
All majors are open to WUE-eligible students.

## Air travel information
Five airports are between one and two and a half hours away. Students usually fly to the least expensive airport and rent a car or find a ride to campus. Salt Lake City airport has a bus service that goes to Dillon; the bus stop is about 1.5 miles from campus.

## Transfer information
GPA of 2.7 and all majors are eligible for WUE.

## Contact information
admissions@umwestern.edu

## Insights from admissions
*The University of Montana Western is the only public institution that operates on a block scheduling model called Experience One in which students take one class at a time for three and a half weeks. Experience One allows you to concentrate on one class at a time and get more out of your education.*

## Insights from others
*UM Western is located in rural Montana, not far from Yellowstone. It's a place where students can experience a true small college experience. They differentiate themselves in that they are one of the few colleges in the country with a block system where students take one class at a time for three and a half weeks. UM Western is also one of, if not the very, lowest-cost WUE colleges.*
  *Brian Swan*
  *Greatland College Consulting*
  *Anchorage, AK*

Nevada has three WUE colleges. University of Nevada, Las Vegas (UNLV) is the largest of the two well-known WUE schools in Nevada, the University of Nevada-Reno being the other. Nevada State University is the state's newest and smallest WUE college. Just north of Las Vegas, it has no on-campus housing.

# WUE Colleges in
# nevada

The Savvy Guide to the 4-Year WUE Colleges

# Nevada State University

Henderson, NV (pop. 175,381) near Las Vegas
www.nsc.nevada.edu

## Overview

**Nevada State University** places a special emphasis on the advancement of a diverse and largely underserved student population. In this role, the institution emphasizes high-quality instruction, exemplary service, engaging learning experiences, and innovation as a means to more efficient, effective outcomes in all corners of the campus..

## Current students

Full time undergraduates . 2,087
WUE students . . . . . . 62/3%
Freshmen out of state . . . . 2%
Freshmen in housing . . . . NR
(public transportation available)
All students in housing . . . 8%
Freshman retention . . . . . 76%
Four-year graduation rate. . NR
Six-year graduation rate. . .28%

## Deadline

February 1

## Admissions

Acceptance rate . . . . . . .70%
ACT median range . . . . . NR
SAT median range. . . . . . NR
Grade-point average. . . . .2.75

## WUE costs

WUE tuition . . . . . . .$10,972
Average R & B* . . . . .$12,000
Mandatory fees . . . . . . . .$0
Other . . . . . . . . . . . $4,000
COA . . . . . . . . . .$26,972
*estimate as college provides housing only, private kitchen for meals.

## WUE requirements and procedures

WUE is automatically awarded upon admission and filling out the residency form.

## Required/recommended high school coursework

- English . . . . . . 4 years
- Math . . . . . . . 3 years   with at least 2 being algebra 1 or higher
- Social studies . . . 3 years
- Science . . . . . . 2 years   one with lab

# Nevada

## Eligible majors
All majors are open to WUE-eligible students.

## Air travel information
Public transportation is available from the Las Vegas airport to the campus.

## Transfer information
2.0 GPA and at least 12 transferable credits and all majors are WUE eligible.

## Contact information
admissions@nsc.edu

## Insights from others
*Nevada State University is located in Henderson, NV, which is a quick 25-minute drive to the Las Vegas Strip. NSU is a teaching-focused university that provides small class sizes and personal attention from professors. Popular majors are nursing and education.*
   *Hailee DeMott*
   *DeMott College & Education*
   *Consulting*
   *Las Vegas, NV*

The Savvy Guide to the 4-Year WUE Colleges

# University of Nevada – Las Vegas

Las Vegas, NV (pop. 603,488)   www.unlv.edu

## Overview

At **UNLV**, we are entrepreneurial and innovative, a place where you can learn, grow, and become something you've never imagined. Our location in Las Vegas offers a living laboratory where you can get hands-on experience in your future career while making a difference in a thriving community. **UNLV** is among the top 3 percent of universities in the nation classified by the Carnegie Classification of Institutions of Higher Education as R1 "very high research activity" status—the gold standard for university research metrics. **UNLV** prides itself in its innovative academics, real-world experience, and undergraduate research opportunities.

## Current students

Full time undergraduates 19,523
WUE students . . . . 1,670/9%
Freshmen out of state . . . . 14%
Freshmen in housing . . . . 18%
All students in housing . . . 5%
Freshman retention . . . . . 77%
Four-year graduation rate. . 18%
Six-year graduation rate. . . 47%

## Deadline

Priority Deadline November 15, Application deadline June 1

## Admissions

Acceptance rate . . . . . . . 83%
ACT median range . . . . 18-25
SAT median range. . . 990-1200
Grade-point average. . . . . 3.4

## WUE costs

WUE tuition . . . . . . . $15,294
Average R & B. . . . . . $13,194
Mandatory fees . . . . . . . . $0
Other . . . . . . . . . . . $4,000
COA . . . . . . . . . . . $32,488

## Required/recommended high school coursework

- English . . . . . . 4 years
- Math . . . . . . . 3 years   algebra 1 & 2, geometry, trigonometry, pre-calculus, probability and statistics or other advanced math
- Social studies . . . 3 years
- Science . . . . . . 3 years   2 must be lab sciences

# Nevada

## WUE requirements and procedures
Students must have one of the following: 3.25 GPA Or 24 ACT Or 1160 SAT.

## Eligible majors
All majors are open to WUE-eligible students.

## Air travel information
Airport is seven miles away. Taxi/Uber/Lyft are the easiest ways to get to campus.

## Transfer information
3.0 GPA and no more than 90 transfer credits.

## Contact information
admissions@unlv.edu

### Insights from admissions
*We recommend that students apply and get admitted early, prior to our priority deadline for consideration for scholarships. Doing so gives students the best chance possible to get awarded scholarship funds (outside of WUE) before the funding runs out.*

### Insights from others
*UNLV is an academic oasis on the outskirts of Las Vegas, allowing students to experience a large research university coupled with countless internships. In addition to the more traditional academic pursuits, UNLV takes full advantage of the many entertainment and hospitality industry resources including majors ranging from hospitality to theater to mechanical engineering. As a member of the NCAA Division I, Rebels can have the big college sports experience.*
*Sue Zoby*
*Mission Admission*
*Denver, CO*

The Savvy Guide to the 4-Year WUE Colleges

# University of Nevada – Reno

Reno, NV (pop. 232,294)
www.unr.edu

## Overview

Our students come here for a number of reasons, but on the top of that list is the high quality education we provide. We're proud to be recognized as a national Tier 1 University by "U.S. New & World Report." The university's continued ranking in the top tier is a statement about the students we attract, the graduates we produce, the quality of our faculty and their world-improving research and creativity. All this in a great setting and with Division I sports!

## Current students

Full time undergraduates 16,951
WUE students . . . . 2,723/16%
Freshmen out of state . . . . 24%
Freshmen in housing . . . . 68%
All students in housing . . . 18%
Freshman retention . . . . . 79%
Four-year graduation rate. . 40%
Six-year graduation rate. . . 63%

## Deadline

Early action deadline November 15; final deadline April 7.

## Admissions

Acceptance rate . . . . . . . 86%
ACT median range . . . . 19-26
SAT median range. . 1060-1280
Grade-point average. . . . . 3.4

## WUE costs

WUE tuition . . . . . . . $12,814
Average R & B. . . . . . $14,700
Mandatory fees . . . . . $1,654
Other . . . . . . . . . . . $4,000
COA . . . . . . . . . . . $33,168

## Required/recommended high school coursework

- English . . . . . . 4 years
- Math . . . . . . . 3 years   algebraa and higher
- Social studies . . . 3 years
- Science . . . . . . 3 years   preferably biology, chemistry and physics, with at least 2 in a laboratory

# Nevada

## WUE requirements and procedures
Students must have one of the following; 3.25 GPA Or 24 ACT Or 1160 SAT. Freshman are encouraged to live on-campus during their first year..

## Eligible majors
All majors are open to WUE-eligible students.

## Air travel information
Reno has a regional airport. Taxi/Uber/Lyft are the easiest ways to get to campus.

## Transfer information
3.0 GPA and have 24 transferable semester credits.

## Contact information
admissions@unr.edu

## Insights from others
*UNR is a great option for a student seeking a student-centered college with a diverse student body and a wide range of majors. There are no impacted programs and support is provided for undecided students. It has a large commuter population, but there are many initiatives to help students feel more connected to the campus community. UNR offers numerous undergrad research opportunities, and works with local corporations to develop educational programs that prepare graduates to be successful in their field.*
*Nicole Houseman*
*On My Way Consulting*
*Berkeley, CA*

## Insights from admissions
*The University of Nevada, Reno is a flagship land-grant institution, recognized as a Best Global University by U.S. News & World Report, a Carnegie R1 research university, and offers an unparalleled tuition rate. We have made history with the most academically prepared and culturally diverse class to date. With over 20,000 students from all 50 states and across the globe, our institution continues to break records and attract top talent.*

New Mexico

New Mexico has seven four-year WUE schools. The two large ones are New Mexico State University and the University of New Mexico. There are three smaller universities. New Mexico Western and New Mexico Highlands are open-enrollment universities, while Eastern New Mexico University is not. New Mexico Tech is also a smaller school that focuses on technology. Northern New Mexico College generally has no WUE students and is not included.

# WUE Colleges in
# new mexico

The Savvy Guide to the 4-Year WUE Colleges

# Eastern New Mexico University

Portales, NM (pop. 12,497)
www.enmu.edu

## Overview

At **Eastern New Mexico University**, you'll get the personal attention you need to succeed in college and in life. Whatever you choose to study, we've got you covered. Our professors know you by name and take time to answer your questions. ENMU is in the top 10 percent of the most affordable public southwestern four-year universities. At **Eastern**, we focus on preparing you for professional and personal success with a quality education. With more than 50 student organizations, you'll find friends and have the opportunity to get involved in academic, cultural, multicultural, service, special interest, and fraternity or sorority events.

## Current students

Full time undergraduates . 1,016
WUE students . . . . . . 90 / 6%
Freshmen out of state . . . . .17%
Freshmen in housing . . . . .73%
All students in housing . . .20%
Freshman retention . . . . NR%
Four-year graduation rate. .24%
Six-year graduation rate. . .41%

## Admissions

Acceptance rate . . . . . . .95%
ACT median range . . . . 15-23
SAT median range. . . . . . NR
Grade-point average. . . . . 3.3

## WUE costs

WUE tuition . . . . . . . $6,174
Average R & B. . . . . . $8,856

### Insights from admissions

For freshman students we offer academic scholarships based on ACT or SAT scores. These begin at 20 ACT or 940 SAT. Freshmen can also receive in-state tuition rate on top of the academic scholarships by having a 3.0 high school GPA and a 23 ACT (1060 SAT) or a 3.5 high school GPA and a 20 ACT (940 SAT). We also offer transfer scholarships; these begin at a 3.5 cumulative GPA. This will give transfer students our in-state tuition rate and a scholarship.

New Mexico

Mandatory fees . . . . . $2,880
Other . . . . . . . . . . . $4,000
COA . . . . . . . . . . . .$21,910

### Deadline
August 1

### WUE requirements and procedures
WUE is automatically awarded upon admission.

### Required/recommended high school coursework
None

### Eligible majors
All majors are open to WUE-eligible students.

### Air travel information
Nearest major airports are at Lubbock, TX and Amarillo, TX, both about an hour and a half. Renting a car is the best option.

### Transfer information
Transfers are eligible for WUE.

### Contact information
enrollment.services@enmu.edu

### Insights from others
*ENMU thinks of itself more as a mentoring institution than a university—although it does have some excellent programs including education and criminal justice. Many students are comfortable here because of its small size. It has a genuine, friendly feel and is fairly conservative. It's a place where a student can be nurtured without the pressure that comes in many universities.*
*Glenda Durano*
*College Advising and Planning Services*
*Albuquerque, NM*

# New Mexico Highlands University

Las Vegas, NM (pop. 13,691)
www.enmu.edu

## Overview

**New Mexico Highlands University** is nestled against the foothill of the Sangre de Cristo Mountains in the historic city of Las Vegas, New Mexico. NMHU offers the most affordable four-year tuition in the United States, topping the list as one of the most affordable public universities in the United States, according to "US News & World Report." Our small student population and historic rural desert mountain locale create a balanced setting that allows you to focus on your pursuits, easily form friendships and collaborations, and do what you've set out to do while featuring a twelve-to-one student-faculty ratio, truly unique for a public university!

## Current students

Full time undergraduates . 1,016
WUE students . . . . . . 90/9%
Freshmen out of state . . . .17%
Freshmen in housing . . . .73%
All students in housing . . .20%
Freshman retention . . . . . NR
Four-year graduation rate. . 24%
Six-year graduation rate. . . 41%

## Deadline

Second Friday after classes start

## Admissions

Acceptance rate . . . . . . .95%
ACT median range . . . . 15-23
SAT median range. . . . . . NR
Grade-point average. . . . . 3.3

## WUE costs

WUE tuition . . . . . . .$10,920
Average R & B. . . . . .$11,436
Mandatory fees . . . . . . . .$0
Other . . . . . . . . . . . $4,000
COA . . . . . . . . . . .$26,356

## WUE requirements and procedures

WUE is automatically awarded upon admission.

## Required/recommended high school coursework

No specific coursework is required.

## Eligible majors

All majors are open to WUE-eligible students.

## Air travel information

The closest airport is about two hours away in Albuquerque. The student must find a ride to campus; the school does not offer transportation.

## Transfer information

2.0 GPA and be eligible for WUE.

## Contact information

admissions@nmhu.edu

The Savvy Guide to the 4-Year WUE Colleges

# New Mexico State University

Las Cruces, NM (pop. 101,324)
www.nmsu.edu

## Overview

Explore the many exciting opportunities to shape your future at **New Mexico State University**. Here, you will gain experience and know-how that will prepare you to lead the next generation of scientists, engineers, business and health care professionals, scholars and teachers. You will learn from and work alongside top-notch faculty and researchers at the helm of our 21st-century fields of study. An Hispanic serving institution, **NMSU** serves a multi-cultural population of students with its main campus in beautiful Albuquerque, where students can explore the city and the great outdoors while our Division I sports team provide a great sense of pride.

## Current students

Full time undergraduates . . 9,322
WUE students . . . . . 181/2%
Freshmen out of state . . . .26%
Freshmen in housing . . . .56%
All students in housing . . .23%
Freshman retention . . . . .73%
Four-year graduation rate. . .23%
Six-year graduation rate. . .51%

## Admissions

Acceptance rate . . . . . . .78%
ACT median range . . . . 17-23
SAT median range. . . 900-1140
Grade-point average. . . . .3.52

## WUE costs

WUE tuition . . . . . . .$11,868
Average R & B. . . . . .$11,555
Mandatory fees . . . . . . . .$0
Other . . . . . . . . . . . $4,000
COA . . . . . . . . . . .$27,423

## Deadline

March 1. There is no deadline for students to receive our WUE tuition discount.

## WUE requirements and procedures

WUE is automatically awarded upon admission.

## Required/recommended high school coursework

None is required.

# New Mexico

## Eligible majors
All majors are open to WUE-eligible students.

## Air travel information
Best option is to fly to El Paso International Airport and rent a car.

## Transfer information
2.0 GPA and 24 completed credit hours.

## Contact information
admissions@nmsu.edu

## Insights from admissions
*At New Mexico State University, we believe out-of-state tuition doesn't have to be expensive, which is why we proudly participate in the WUE program to offer affordable tuition rates to eligible students. Students from participating states can take advantage of our exemplary academic programs, exceptional educational value, and our diverse and vibrant campus community. Take the next steps toward success and join us at NMSU!*

## Insights from others
*Like most "state" schools, NMSU has a strong Agriculture Department, including a wine program. The school also offers good engineering opportunities and has excellent media facilities. NMSU has a smaller community feel than larger state schools, but it has all the standard offerings. It would be an excellent school for students who want the advantages of a large, state school but don't want the urban feel.*
  Glenda Durano
  College Advising and Planning Services
  Albuquerque, NM

# New Mexico Tech

Socorro, NM (pop. 8,911)
www.nmt.edu

## Overview

**New Mexico Tech** is unique, in that it is a small college that is looking for students who are intrigued by math, science, engineering, and technology. **NMT** is one hour south of Albuquerque. Hands-on learners do especially well at **Tech** due to the abundance of research opportunities that take theoretical classroom learning and apply it to research, lab work, and field experience.

## Current students

Full time undergraduates . 1,093
WUE students . . . . . . 16/2%
Freshmen out of state . . . . 10%
Freshmen in housing . . . . 88%
All students in housing . . . 78%
Freshman retention . . . . . 75%
Four-year graduation rate. . 38%
Six-year graduation rate. . . 50%

## Admissions

Acceptance rate . . . . . . . 75%
ACT median range . . . . 21-28
SAT median range. . 1110-1320
Grade-point average. . . . . 3.65

## WUE costs

WUE tuition . . . . . . . $14,270
Average R & B. . . . . $10,350
Mandatory fees . . . . . . . . $0
Other . . . . . . . . . . . . $4000
COA . . . . . . . . . . . $28,620

## Deadline

March 1.

## WUE requirements and procedures

3.0 GPA and 23 ACT or 1130 SAT.

## Required/recommended high school coursework

None, but taking at least pre-calculus in math is strongly recommended.

## Eligible majors

All majors are open to WUE-eligible students.

# New Mexico

## Air travel information
Car rentals are available from the Albuquerque International Sunport (airport). A combination of shuttle service and trams will get you to campus, but most students can get rides when needed.

## Transfer information
Transfer students with a GPA of 3.0 and 30 transferable hours are eligible for all majors.

## Contact information
admission@admin.nmt.edu

The Savvy Guide to the 4-Year WUE Colleges

# University of New Mexico

Albuquerque, NM (pop. 552,804)
www.unm.edu

## Overview

**The University of New Mexico** in Albuquerque is home to 25,000 students from every state in the union and almost every country in the world. New Mexico's comprehensive flagship institution, **UNM** offers more than 200 degree programs in 13 respected colleges and schools.

## Current students

Full time undergraduates  13,745
WUE students . . . . . 369/3%
Freshmen out of state . . . . .21%
Freshmen in housing . . . .50%
All students in housing . . .23%
Freshman retention . . . . .72%
Four-year graduation rate. . .33%
Six-year graduation rate. . .50%

## Admissions

Acceptance rate . . . . . . .79%
ACT median range . . . . 19-26
SAT median range. . . 910-1150
Grade-point average. . . . . 3.4

## WUE costs

WUE tuition* . . . . . .$11,445
Average R & B. . . . . .$11,993
Mandatory fees . . . . . . . .$0
Other . . . . . . . . . . . $4,000
COA . . . . . . . . . . .$27,438

*This is the same as an in-state student since a 3.0 GPA qualifies for in-state tuition.

## Deadline

February 1

## WUE requirements and procedures

2.8 GPA OR 18 ACT. *NOTE: students with a 3.0 GPA OR ACT 20 pay in-state tuition.

## Required/recommended high school coursework

- English . . . . . . 4 years  with at least 1 composition course in the 11th or 12th grade
- Math . . . . . . . 4 years  algebra 1 & 2, geometry, pre-calculus or trigonometry or statistics
- Social studies . . . 3 years  1 should be US history

# New Mexico

- Science . . . . . . 3 years  2 should be lab sciences such as biology, chemistry or physics
- Foreign language . 2 years  of the same language

## Eligible majors
All majors are open to WUE-eligible students.

## Air travel information
Public buses run from the Albuquerque International Sunport (airport) to campus. It's about a three-mile trip.

## Transfer information
2.8 GPA and at least 30 credit hours.

## Contact information
unmlobos@unm.edu

## Insights from others
*UNM has bragging rights as the state's flagship university. Many of the students are from New Mexico, but the school tries to attract out-of-staters by offering generous scholarships. Although the school is large, it boasts of community; students, however, must "dig in" and take advantage of the opportunities such as LLCs and the Freshman Learning Experience. Some of UNM's unique/stronger programs include an Emergency Academy with a specialty in mountain/skiing medicine, a BA/MD program, Flamenco dancing, and any field of study that emphasizes the Latin cultures.*
Glenda Durano
College Advising and
Planning Services
Albuquerque, NM

The Savvy Guide to the 4-Year WUE Colleges

# Western New Mexico University

Silver City, NM (pop. 10,273)
www.wnmu.edu

## Overview

**Western New Mexico University** is in Silver City, surrounded by the Gila National Forest in a beautiful mountain environment along the Continental Divide. **Western New Mexico** has a student enrollment of approximately 2,800 and offers undergraduate programs in business, education, liberal arts, the sciences and vocational education. Some graduate degree programs in business administration and education are also offered.

## Current students

| | |
|---|---|
| Full time undergraduates | 1,851 |
| WUE students | 53/3% |
| Freshmen out of state | 30% |
| Freshmen in housing | 40% |
| All students in housing | 10% |
| Freshman retention | 71% |
| Four-year graduation rate | 19% |
| Six-year graduation rate | 29% |

## Admissions

| | |
|---|---|
| Acceptance rate | 99% |
| ACT median range | NR |
| SAT median range | NR |
| Grade-point average | 2.5 |

## Deadline

August 1

## WUE costs

| | |
|---|---|
| WUE tuition | $9,820 |
| Average R & B | $10,940 |
| Mandatory fees | $0 |
| Other | $4,000 |
| COA | $24,760 |

## Insights from admissions

*We are especially proud of our pass rate of 100 percent for the NCAT through our School of Nursing! We have students who come from afar for our social work, business, and nursing programs. Nursing is available to WUE students.*

## WUE requirements and procedures

WUE is automatically awarded upon admission.

# New Mexico

## Required/recommended high school coursework
None. This is an open enrollment university.

## Eligible majors
All majors are open to WUE-eligible students.

## Air travel information
Students usually fly to Tucson, El Paso, or Alburquerque. Rental cars are available at those airports. A bus runs from Tuscon, AZ to Deming, NM, where a shuttle bus connects to Silver City. Whiskey Creek is a regional airport that is a short taxi ride to campus.

## Transfer information
Transfers are eligible for WUE and all majors.

## Contact information
admissions@wnmu.edu

North Dakota

North Dakota has six four-year WUE colleges. The four smaller ones have fewer than than 3,000 full-time undergraduate students enrolled. North Dakota State and the University of North Dakota are larger universities. As of 2024, the University of North Dakota is once again a WUE college. All majors offered are WUE eligible in all six colleges.

# WUE Colleges in
# north
# dakota

The Savvy Guide to the 4-Year WUE Colleges

# Dickinson State University

Dickinson, ND (pop. 20,826)
100 miles north of Bismarck
www.dickinsonstate.edu

## Overview

**Dickinson State University**, with an enrollment of over 1,300 students, is in Dickinson, minutes from the beautiful Badlands. Our location provides abundant opportunities for students to enjoy numerous outdoor recreational activities year round. The University provides high-quality, accessible programs; promotes excellence in teaching and learning; supports scholarly and creative activities; and provides services relevant to economy, health and quality of life.

## Current students

Full time undergraduates . 1,398
WUE students . . . . . 142/10%
Freshmen out of state . . . . 37%
Freshmen in housing . . . 100%
All students in housing . . . 28%
Freshman retention . . . . . 71%
Four-year graduation rate . . 19%
Six-year graduation rate . . . 39%

## Deadline

August 1

## Required/recommended high school coursework

- English . . . . . . 4 years
- Math . . . . . . . 3 years   algebra 1 and above
- Social studies . . . 3 years
- Science . . . . . . 3 years   at least one unit each in two or more of the following: biology, chemistry, physics or physical science

## Admissions

Acceptance rate . . . . . . . 66%
ACT median range . . . . 16-21
SAT median range . . . 875-1130
Grade-point average . . . . . 3.28

## WUE costs

WUE tuition* . . . . . . $8,288
Average R & B . . . . . . $8,822
Mandatory fees . . . . . $1,648
Other . . . . . . . . . . . $4,000
COA . . . . . . . . . . . $22,758

*This is the same as an in-state student as WUE-state students receive in-state tuition.

North Dakota

## WUE requirements and procedures
2.0 GPA.

## Eligible majors
All majors are open to WUE-eligible students.

## Air travel information
Taxi/Uber/Lyft or bus service is available from the airport to campus..

## Transfer information
WUE is available to all transfer students with at least 24 transferable semester credits.

## Contact information
dsu.hawk@dickinsonstate.edu

## Insights from admissions
*Choosing to attend college is a momentous decision. Whether your plan involves a two or four-year degree or you are pursuing a certificate program, you will find that DSU's low tuition, impressive job placement rates, and wide range of academic programs provide a solid starting point for a variety of outcomes. The staff in admissions, financial aid, and international programs are here to help you through the admissions process. Contact us today to learn more..*

The Savvy Guide to the 4-Year WUE Colleges

# Mayville State University

Mayville, ND (pop. 1,858) 55 miles north of Fargo
www.mayvillestate.edu

## Overview

**Mayville State University** is in the Red River Valley of eastern North Dakota. The faculty and staff of **Mayville State University**, known as "The School of Personal Service," take great pride in providing exceptional personal assistance to all students during their college experience. The campus has a laptop computer requirement for all students and uniform software licensing to enable the student to effectively use technology in and out of the classroom. MSU offers small class sizes and a low student-to-faculty ratio. All students have opportunities to participate in exciting extracurricular activities, everything from varsity sports to music and theater, student government, and much more.

## Current students

Full time undergraduates . . 560
WUE students . . . . . 61/11%
Freshmen out of state . . . .30%
Freshmen in housing . . . .11%
All students in housing . . .10%
Freshman retention . . . . .61%
Four-year graduation rate. .17%
Six-year graduation rate. . .35%

## Deadline

No firm deadline

## Admissions

Acceptance rate . . . . . . .95%
ACT median range . . . . 17-23
SAT median range. . . . . . NR
Grade-point average. . . . .3.14

## WUE costs

WUE tuition* . . . . . . $9,152
Average R & B. . . . . . $8,237
Mandatory fees . . . . . $1,465
Other . . . . . . . . . . . $4,000
COA . . . . . . . . . . .$22,853

*Out-of-state tuition is less than 150% of in-state tuition

## Required/recommended high school coursework

- English . . . . . . 4 years
- Math . . . . . . . 3 years   algebra 1 and above
- Social studies . . . 3 years
- Science . . . . . . 3 years

# North Dakota

## WUE requirements and procedures
GPA of 2.5 OR ACT of 18 or SAT 940.

## Eligible majors
All majors are open to WUE eligible students.

## Air travel information
Nearest commercial airports are in Grand Forks and Fargo.

## Transfer information
GPA of 2.5

## Contact information
askus@mayvillestate.edu

### Insights from admissions
*Mayville State University guarantees the WUE price. We are one of the most affordable four year schools in the country! From on-campus to on-line, check out what Mayville State University has to offer.*

The Savvy Guide to the 4-Year WUE Colleges

# Minot State University

Minot, ND (pop. 46,321)
www.minotstate.edu

## Overview

**Minot State University** is in north central North Dakota, in the heart of Minot, and offers tons of areas of study, state-of-the-art technology in and out the classroom, and in-state tuition for all students! At Minot State, you will join a community that values inclusivity and fosters leadership. You'll forge connections and skills for your future with our 11:1 student-to-professor ratio, hands-on-learning, collaborative experiences tied to your programs of study, and numerous internship opportunities. You will leave here career ready, as over 96 percent of our recent grads are employed or obtaining higher education. This is a place for you to call home—a community where you'll establish lifelong connections.

## Current students

Full time undergraduates . 1,767
WUE students . . . . . 327/19%
Freshmen out of state . . . . .28%
Freshmen in housing . . . . .53%
All students in housing . . .16%
Freshman retention . . . . .70%
Four-year graduation rate. . .23%
Six-year graduation rate. . .46%

## Deadline

Rolling admissions

## Admissions

Acceptance rate . . . . . . .93%
ACT median range . . . . 17-23
SAT median range. . . 990-1180
Grade-point average. . . . .3.46

## WUE costs

WUE tuition* . . . . . . $7,598
Average R & B. . . . . . $9,420
Mandatory fees . . . . . $1,594
Other . . . . . . . . . . . $4,000
COA . . . . . . . . . . . .$22,612

*This is the same as an in-state student, as WUE-state students receive in-state tuition.

## WUE requirements and procedures

WUE is automatically awarded upon admission.

# North Dakota

### Required/recommended high school coursework
- English . . . . . . 4 years
- Math . . . . . . . 3 years algebra 1 and above; excludes business, consumer and general math.
- Social studies . . . 3 years
- Science . . . . . . 3 years at least 2 of biology, chemistry, physics or physical science

### Eligible majors
All majors are open to WUE-eligible students

### Air travel information
Minot international airport (MOT) is nearby.

### Transfer information
Transfers are eligible for WUE

### Contact information
askmsu@minotstateu.edu

### Insights from admissions
*Out-of-state students pay the same as in-state students!*

# North Dakota State University

Fargo, ND (pop. 113,658)
www.ndsu.edu

## Overview

**North Dakota State University** is a student-focused research university with more than 14,000 students from forty-seven states and seventy-nine countries, creating a diverse student population. Programs are academically rigorous, but more than 70 percent of our classes have forty or fewer students, creating an immersive learning environment in which our faculty are committed to student success. The campus offers excellent facilities for living, learning and making lifelong connections.

## Current students

Full time undergraduates . . 8,902
WUE students . . . . . 340/4%
Freshmen out of state . . . .65%
Freshmen in housing . . . .93%
All students in housing . . .37%
Freshman retention . . . . .75%
Four-year graduation rate. . .43%
Six-year graduation rate. . .63%

## Admissions

Acceptance rate . . . . . . .95%
ACT median range . . . . 19-25
SAT median range. . 1000-1200
Grade-point average. . . . . 3.5

## WUE costs

WUE tuition . . . . . . .$14,802
Average R & B. . . . . .$10,378
Mandatory fees . . . . . $1,669
Other . . . . . . . . . . . $4,000
COA . . . . . . . . . . .$30,849

## Deadline

August 15, but incoming freshmen are encouraged to apply by January

## Required/recommended high school coursework

- English . . . . . . 4 years
- Math . . . . . . . 3 years   algebra 1 and above
- Social studies . . . 3 years
- Science . . . . . . 3 years
- Plus one additional class from those above or a foreign language

# North Dakota

## WUE requirements and procedures
WUE is automatically awarded upon admission.

## Eligible majors
All majors are open to WUE eligible students.

## Air travel information
Fargo airport.

## Transfer information
2.0 GPA is recommended, all majors are WUE eligible

## Contact information
ndsu.admission@ndsu.edu

### Insights from admissions
*As a student at NDSU, you will find yourself exchanging ideas with classmates, putting theories to the test in high tech laboratories, presenting solutions to business problems in executive boardrooms, and practicing life-saving skills in clinical settings. As a regional hub for arts, culture and recreation, Fargo-Moorhead combines small town friendliness with the cultural offerings of a large city. With a metropolitan area population of nearly 200,000, Fargo-Moorhead is the largest community between Minneapolis and Seattle and is regularly recognized by national publications and surveys for its great job opportunities, safety and recreational opportunities.*

The Savvy Guide to the 4-Year WUE Colleges

# University of North Dakota

Grand Forks, ND (pop. 60,000), right on the Minnesota state line.
www.und.edu

## Overview

Founded in 1883, six years before the state itself was established, **UND** gave North Dakota its name when the former Dakota territories separated into two distinct states. Today, **UND** is a busy 521-acre campus, the state's largest. Our enrollment continues to grow, defying national trends. We've emerged as a leader in engineering, medicine, aviation, space, and unmanned aircraft systems..

## Current students

Full time undergraduates . 6,991
WUE students . . . . . 549/8%
Freshmen out of state . . . .62%
Freshmen in housing . . . .89%
All students in housing . . .24%
Freshman retention . . . . .79%
Four-year graduation rate. .47%
Six-year graduation rate. . .63%

## Insights from admissions

*Applying for the WUE tuition rate is easy and seamless. Just apply online using our online application. We take care of the rest.*

## Admissions

Acceptance rate . . . . . . .83%
ACT median range . . . . 20-26
SAT median range. . 1100-1280
Grade-point average. . . . . 3.6

## WUE costs

WUE tuition* . . . . . .$14,687
Average R & B. . . . . .$11,758
Mandatory fees . . . . . $1,854
Other . . . . . . . . . . . $4,000
COA . . . . . . . . . . .$32,299

*Out-of-state tuition is less than 150 percent of in-state tuition.

# North Dakota

## Deadline
August 1, but February 1 is the deadline for priority scholarships

## Required/Recommended high school coursework
- English . . . . . . 4 units
- Math . . . . . . . 3 units of Algebra I or above
- Lab Science. . . . 3 units
- Social Studies. . . 3 units
- 1 additional unit from English, math, lab science or social studies, or world language (including foreign languages, Native American languages or American Sign Language)

## WUE requirements and procedures
WUE is automatically awarded upon admission

## Eligible majors
All majors are open to WUE-eligible students except the aerospace/aviation program.

## Air travel information
Fly into Grand Forks International Airport and then taxi/Uber/Lyft to campus.

## Transfer information
All majors are WUE eligible except the aerospace/aviation Program

## Contact information
admissions@und.edu

# Valley City State University

Valley City, ND (pop. 6,699) 58 miles west of Fargo
www.vcsu.edu

## Overview

**Valley City State University** leads with a student-focused, learning-centered approach, offering more than 80 degree programs and enabling its students to thrive in a personable, accessible and affordable environment. Its small, beautiful campus provides students with plentiful opportunities for close connections with fellow students, faculty and staff, and for participation in a complete range of student activities and NAIA athletic programs. One of the first "laptop universities" in the nation, **VCSU** continues its innovative use of technology in all areas of study.

## Current students

Full time undergraduates . 1,526
WUE students . . . . . 143/9%
Freshmen out of state . . . .37%
Freshmen in housing . . . .95%
All students in housing . . .32%
Freshman retention . . . . .70%
Four-year graduation rate. .28%
Six-year graduation rate. . .44%

## Admissions

Acceptance rate . . . . . . .85%
ACT median range . . . . 17-23
SAT median range. . . . . . NR
Grade-point average. . . . .3.38

## WUE costs

WUE tuition* . . . . . . $8,729
Average R & B. . . . . . $7,950
Mandatory fees . . . . . $2,027
Other . . . . . . . . . . . $4,000
COA . . . . . . . . . .$22,706

### Insights from admissions

*VCSU enhances the learning experience by providing full-time students with access to their own laptop, advanced multimedia technology, high-speed wireless networking, and classrooms equipped with the latest educational technology. A student-faculty ratio of about 13:1 gives students individual access to faculty in ways that are impossible at other universities.*

*Out-of-state tuition is less than 150 percent of in-state-tuition.

# North Dakota

## Deadline
The beginning of each semester

## Required/recommended high school coursework
- English . . . . . . 4 years
- Math . . . . . . . 3 years  algebra 1 and above
- Social studies . . . 3 years
- Science . . . . . . 3 years

## WUE requirements and procedures
WUE is automatically awarded upon admission.

## Eligible majors
All majors are open to WUE-eligible students

## Air travel information
Students will fly into Fargo's Hector International Airport. Taxi rides can be set up for transportation from airport to campus. Run by the Valley City South Central Transit Service, the taxi is available for in town or trips out of town. A taxi ride to or from Fargo, at any time of day or night, costs $65. That fare can be shared by multiple riders. Early-morning rides such to catch a 5 AM or 6 AM flight from Fargo must be arranged at least one day in advance. To line up rides or for further information call South Central Transit Services at 701-845-4300. Uber and Lyft are options as well.

## Transfer information
GPA of 2.00 and at least 24 transferable credits eligible for WUE tuition

## Contact information
enrollment.services@vcsu.edu

Oregon

Of the state's two biggest and best-known schools, the University of Oregon is NOT part of WUE, but Oregon State has recently joined. Eastern Oregon University is a small WUE school. Southern Oregon University is small to medium sized and Western Oregon University is the largest outside of Portland. Portland State University is Oregon's largest WUE college and the only Oregon WUE school in a large metropolitan area. It also has many commuters and evening students. Oregon Tech, as its name implies, is a polytechnic university.

# WUE Colleges in
# oregon

The Savvy Guide to the 4-Year WUE Colleges

# Eastern Oregon University

La Grade, OR (pop. 13,048)
www.eou.edu

## Overview

**Eastern Oregon University** offers a premier small-college educational experience at the price of a public university. The campus is minutes away from skiing, rafting, and other outdoor opportunities. EOU is a place with highly ranked academics, where students and staff get to know each other and build lasting relationships that create possibilities to succeed in school and beyond.

## Current students

Full time undergraduates . 1,469
WUE students . . . . . 189/13%
Freshmen out of state . . . . .31%
Freshmen in housing . . . .74%
All students in housing . . .14%
Freshman retention . . . . .68%
Four-year graduation rate. . .28%
Six-year graduation rate. . .38%

## Admissions

Acceptance rate . . . . . . .99%
ACT median range . . . . 17-23
SAT median range. . . 940-1140
Grade-point average. . . . .3.46

## WUE costs

WUE tuition . . . . . . .$14,175
Average R & B. . . . . .$12,534
Mandatory fees . . . . . $1,215
Other . . . . . . . . . . . $4,000
COA . . . . . . . . . . . .$31,927

## Insights from others

*Because EOU is so far from anywhere, it is a very outdoorsy campus, which attracts lots of hunters. It is the first campus we ever visited that has gun lockers in the dorms. Human Performance with concentrations in Community Health, Nature/Outdoor Rec, & Exercise is a strong major, because of the types of students who attend. Otherwise Business & Education are strong.*
   *Marcia Monma*
   *College Search Consultants*
   *Clinton, WA*

Oregon

## Deadline
September is the general deadline

## Required/recommended high school coursework
- English . . . . . . 4 years
- Math . . . . . . . 3 years   algebra 1 and 2; other math classes that are college preparatory
- Social studies . . . 3 years   1 year US history, 1 year world history or geography, 1 year government recommended
- Science . . . . . . 3 years   2 years college preparatory, 1 year lab science recommended
- Foreign language . 2 years

## WUE requirements and procedures
WUE is automatically awarded upon admission.

## Eligible majors
All majors are open to WUE-eligible students

## Air travel information
La Grande is one hundred twenty-one miles from Tri-Cities Airport in Pasco, WA.

## Transfer information
2.25 GPA and 30 transferable quarter or 20 transferable semester credits.

## Contact information
admissions@eou.edu

### Insights from admissions
*Students from Idaho and Washington automatically qualify for resident tuition rate.*

# Oregon Institute of Technology

Klamath Falls, OR (pop. 21,005) three hours south of Eugene
www.oit.edu

## Overview

The **Oregon Institute of Technology** has its residential campus in Klamath Falls and sites in the Portland area and Salem. It offers degree programs in engineering, information technology, business, health professions, natural sciences and communication studies. **Oregon Tech** offers a quality education with average class size of 17, student-to-faculty ratio of 15:1, and 91 percent of its courses having 30 or fewer students. Within six months of graduation, 97 percent of our graduates are employed or continuing education. Grads earn an average starting salary of about $60,000 per year.

## Current students

Full time undergraduates . 2,103
WUE students . . . . . .326/15%
Freshmen out of state . . . .31%
Freshmen in housing . . . .66%
All students in housing . . .21%
Freshman retention . . . . .72%
Four-year graduation rate. .30%
Six-year graduation rate. . .57%

## Admissions

Acceptance rate . . . . . . .93%
ACT median range . . . . 23-30
SAT median range. . 1050-1265
Grade-point average. . . . . 3.5

## WUE costs

WUE tuition . . . . . . .$18,743
Average R & B. . . . . .$11,904
Mandatory fees . . . . . . . .$0
Other . . . . . . . . . . . $4,000
COA . . . . . . . . . . .$34,647

### Insights from admissions

Oregon Tech is the only polytechnic university in the Pacific Northwest that offers hands-on experience in all of its four-year baccalaureate degree programs. Graduates enjoy a strong success rate of employment in the field that they earned their degree or acceptance into graduate school within six months after commencement. The majority of Oregon Tech programs are WUE eligible for all admitted students. Non-WUE eligible majors are considered for other scholarships and awards.

# Oregon

## Deadline
Three weeks before term starts

## WUE requirements
WUE is automatically awarded upon admission.

## Required/recommended high school coursework
- English . . . . . . 4 years
- Math . . . . . . . 3 years
- Social studies . . . 3 years
- Science . . . . . . 3 years

## Eligible majors
All but pre-clinical lab science, clinical lab science, pre-dental hygiene, dental hygiene, pre-medical imaging technology, medical imaging technology, nursing after acceptance by Oregon Health Sciences University, paramedic education program.

## Air travel information
Shuttles run from the airport in Medford.

## Transfer information
Transfers with at least 36 quarter hours (24 semester hours) and GPA 2.25 and are eligible for WUE.

## Contact information
oregontech.admissions@oit.edu

### Insights from others

*The focus here, where students get the opportunity to work closely with professors, is giving students the opportunity to learn their craft in a hands-in way. Most OIT students, including all students in the medical imaging field (ultrasound, nuclear, x-ray), must perform an externship before they graduate, and many are offered jobs at their externship site. Self-motivated visual learners will do well at OIT. The programs are rigorous and not all students will complete their major.*

*Evelyn Jerome-Alexander*
*Magellan College Counseling*
*Topanga, CA*

## Oregon State University

Corvallis, OR (pop. 60,000) one and a half hours south of Portland
www.oregonstate.edu

### Overview

Oregon State Univeristy is a dynamic community of dreamers, doers, problem-solvers and change-makers. We don't wait for challenges to present themselves—we seek them out and take them on. We welcome students, faculty and staff from every background and perspective into a community where everyone feels seen and heard. We have deep-rooted mindfulness for the natural world and all who depend on it, and together, we apply knowledge, tools and skills to build a better future for all..

### Current students

Full time undergraduates 19,697
WUE students . . . . 1,033/5%
Freshmen out of state . . . . 41%
Freshmen in housing . . . . 88%
All students in housing . . . 18%
Freshman retention . . . . . 87%
Four-year graduation rate. . 46%
Six-year graduation rate. . . 70%

### Deadline

February 1

### Admissions

Acceptance rate . . . . . . . 83%
ACT median range . . . . 22-30
SAT median range. . 1130-1380
Grade-point average. . . . . 3.64

### WUE costs

WUE tuition . . . . . . . $22,869
Average R & B. . . . . . $17,205
Mandatory fees . . . . . . . . $0
Other . . . . . . . . . . . $4,000
COA . . . . . . . . . . . $44,074

### WUE requirements

3.0 GPA minimum, WUE is competitive, around 30% of students who apply for it will be offered the WUE Scholarship. As of 2022-2023, 1033 students were receiving the WUE tuition rate.

### Required/recommended high school coursework

- English . . . . . . . . 4 years
- Math . . . . . . . . . 3 years

- Social studies. . . . . .3 years
- Science . . . . . . . . .3 years
- Math . . . . . . . . .3 years,
    with . . . . . . .4 years encouraged
- Social studies. . . . . .3 years
- Science . . . . . . . . .3 years
- Secondary language . 2 years

## Eligible majors
All majors are open to WUE-eligible students.

## Air travel information
Fly to Portland PDX and then private shuttle (Groome Transportation) to campus. Fifteen shuttles per day at $49 as of 2024.

## Transfer information
3.0 GPA.

## Contact information
osuadmit@oregonstate.edu

## Insights from others
*OSU is one of a handful of large public flagship WUE colleges. Big-time sports and college experiences here. The engineering department is large and Corvallis is a nice college town. Mountains to the east and the ocean to the west are there to play in this pretty, although sometimes rainy area. The honors college is worth a look for those wanting something more in depth.*
*Brian Swan*
*Greatland College Consulting*
*Anchorage, AK.*

# Portland State University

Portland, OR (pop. 603,106)
www.pdx.edu

## Overview

**Portland State University** is Oregon's premier urban research institution. PSU, in the heart of downtown Portland, offers a breadth of academic opportunities and community connections that enhance and support curricula. PSU is nationally recognized for its interdisciplinary approach to general education, innovative community-based learning, and the strength of its academic programs.

## Current students

Full time undergraduates 11,881
WUE students . . . . . 857/7%
Freshmen out of state . . . . .23%
Freshmen in housing . . . .50%
All students in housing . . . 9%
Freshman retention . . . . .73%
Four-year graduation rate. . .29%
Six-year graduation rate. . .54%

## Admissions

Acceptance rate . . . . . . .98%
ACT median range . . . . 17-26
SAT median range. . 1110-1270
Grade-point average. . . . .3.36

## WUE costs

WUE tuition . . . . . . .$18,471
Average R & B. . . . . .$14,280
Mandatory fees . . . . . . . .$0
Other . . . . . . . . . . . $4,000
COA . . . . . . . . . . .$36,751

## Insights from admissions

*Students are automatically considered for WUE at PSU if they apply. Eligibility is based on academic and residency information provided in their application for admission. Other institutional aid must be applied for by submitting the FAFSA or PSU's scholarship application. Portland State is consistently ranked by* U.S. News and World Report *as one of the most innovative universities in the country. Located in downtown Portland, Oregon, PSU emphasizes research and internships with engineering firms as well as major businesses such as Nike, Intel, and Columbia Sportswear.*

# Oregon

## Deadline
February 1. No hard deadline for WUE consideration.

## Required/recommended high school coursework
- English . . . . . . 4 years
- Math . . . . . . . 3 years  culminating with algebra 2
- Social studies . . . 3 years
- Science . . . . . . 3 years  1 year of lab recommended
- Foreign language . 2 years

## WUE requirements and procedures
3.0 cumulative unweighted GPA OR 27 ACT Or 1270 SAT

## Eligible majors
All majors are open to WUE-eligible students

## Air travel information
Students can use the city's transportations system (bus or MAX train), a shuttle, or a taxi to get to campus. MAX serves Portland's airport. Uber/Lyft are also available.

## Transfer information
Transfer students qualify for WUE tuition with 3.0 college GPA.

## Contact information
admissions@pdx.edu

## Insights from others
*If you want to live and go to school in the great city of Portland and have the benefits and many opportunities of attending a large university, you can have those experiences at PSU. Portland State is a large university in a major city and many of its students commute or attend part-time in the evenings. For those who live on campus or nearby and attend full time, it's a place where you can make the college experience you desire.*
   *Brian Swan*
   *Greatland College*
      *Consulting*
   *Anchorage, AK*

The Savvy Guide to the 4-Year WUE Colleges

# Southern Oregon University

Ashland, OR (pop. 20,713)
www.sou.edu

## Overview

**Southern Oregon University** offers a student-faculty ratio of 21:1 and average class size of 25, ideal for undergraduate instruction. Ashland is internationally recognized for the fine and performing arts and is home of the Oregon Shakespeare Festival. In the foothills of the Siskiyou Mountains, SOU is near the Mt. Ashland ski area, Pacific Crest Trail, and the Cascade-Siskiyou National Monument. The U.S. Fish and Wildlife Forensics Laboratory and Schneider Museum of Art are on the 175-acre campus.

## Current students

Full time undergraduates . 2,262
WUE students . . . . . 719/32%
Freshmen out of state . . . . 39%
Freshmen in housing . . . . 72%
All students in housing . . . 70%
Freshman retention . . . . . 66%
Four-year graduation rate. . 34%
Six-year graduation rate. . . 46%

## Deadline

Rolling admissions

## Admissions

Acceptance rate . . . . . . . 94%
ACT median range . . . . 18-26
SAT median range . . . 990-1200
Grade-point average . . . . . 3.4

## WUE costs

WUE tuition . . . . . . . $16,065
Average R & B . . . . . . $18,863
Mandatory fees . . . . . $2,579
Other . . . . . . . . . . . $4,000
COA . . . . . . . . . . . $41,507

## WUE requirements and procedures

WUE is awarded upon admission.

## Required/recommended high school coursework

- English . . . . . . 4 years
- Math . . . . . . . 3 years  algebra 1, geometry, algebra 2
- Social studies . . . 3 years
- Science . . . . . . 3 years  2 years of lab science
- Foreign language . 2 years

# Oregon

## Eligible majors
All majors are open to WUE-eligible students

## Air travel information
Medford airport is the closest airport.

## Transfer information
There are no minimums to apply and WUE is available to transfers.

## Contact information
admissions@sou.edu

### Insights from admissions
*Southern Oregon University's 6,100 students are offered career-focused, comprehensive educational experiences and multiple scholarship opportunities. A scholarship pool called the Southern Oregon Scholarship Application (SOSA) is available to all admitted students. Potential options for students include diversity, first-generation and merit-based scholarships. Various SOU athletic programs and campus departments also offer scholarship opportunities..*

### Insights from others
*Southern Oregon University is a laid-back school that is well-respected in the local area for providing students with a good community and excellent education. The professors are supportive and accessible and the academic environment is non-competitive. The funky college town of Ashland is most known for the annual Shakespeare Festival; naturally the theater program at SOU is quite strong. It's a nice place for a student who loves the outdoors, with frequent excursions to the nearby rivers and mountains. Because it's located in the far southern region of Oregon, the weather is dry and warm in the summer, with some snow in the winter.*
          *Nicole Hosemann*
          *On My Way Consulting*
          *Berkeley, CA*

The Savvy Guide to the 4-Year WUE Colleges

# Western Oregon University

Monmouth, OR (pop. 9,534)
   Twenty miles southwest of Salem
www.wou.edu

## Overview

**Western Oregon University** is a leading comprehensive public university that has received numerous national awards for its academic advising and success in educating students of all backgrounds. In the Monmouth-Independence area, the heart of Oregon's lush Willamette Valley, **WOU** is about twenty minutes from Salem, the state's capital, and is about seventy-five minutes from Portland, the state's cultural hub.

## Current students

Full time undergraduates . 2,446
WUE students . . . . . 532/22%
Freshmen out of state . . . . 37%
Freshmen in housing . . . . 70%
All students in housing . . . 19%
Freshman retention . . . . . 65%
Four-year graduation rate. . 28%
Six-year graduation rate. . . 41%

## Deadline

The first day of classes

## Admissions

Acceptance rate . . . . . . . 93%
ACT median range . . . . 18-26
SAT median range. . . 980-1220
Grade-point average. . . . . 3.4

## WUE costs

WUE tuition . . . . . . . $14,175
Average R & B. . . . . .$12,528
Mandatory fees . . . . . $2,064
Other . . . . . . . . . . . $3,000
COA . . . . . . . . . . . .$32,767

## Required/recommended high school coursework

- English . . . . . . 4 years
- Math . . . . . . . 3 years   culminating with algebra 2 or higher
- Social studies . . . 3 years
- Science . . . . . . 3 years
- Second language . 2 years

## WUE requirements and procedures

WUE is awarded upon admission.

Oregon

## Eligible majors

All majors are open to WUE-eligible students

## Air travel information

From Portland International Airport, students can catch the HUT shuttle to Salem, then the CARTS bus into Monmouth. During peak times, the Student Affairs Office will have a van driving to and from the Portland airport.

## Transfer information

Transfers are eligible for WUE with 36+ quarter hours (24 semester hours) and 2.25 GPA and must have passed college writing and college math.

## Contact information

wolfgram@wou.edu

### Insights from admissions

*WOU's focus, from pricing to class size and academic advising, is on student success. Scholarships and financial aid can be combined with WUE to make the WOU education more affordable than staying in-state. WOU's unique Tuition Choice program allows WUE recipients to select the Tuition Promise, which freezes their tuition rate for four years.*

### Insights from others

*Western Oregon University serves first-generation college students well, and has a very accepting campus for all students. About 80 percent of the students are from Oregon, so it is a bit of a commuter campus, but dorm facilities, including living/learning communities, are modern.*
  *Evelyn Jerome-Alexander*
  *Magellan College Counseling*
  *Topanga, CA*

South Dakota

South Dakota has six four-year WUE schools. Northern State, Dakota State, and Black Hills State are smaller schools. South Dakota State University and the University of South Dakota are medium-sized universities. South Dakota School of Mines & Technology is a STEM college. All the South Dakota schools have an out-of-state tuition rate less than 150% of the in-state tuition, so it's better than the WUE rate. All majors are eligible as well. South Dakota has some of the lower-cost colleges in the west.

# WUE Colleges in
# south
# dakota

The Savvy Guide to the 4-Year WUE Colleges

# Black Hills State University

Spearfish, SD (pop. 10,718) 47 miles from Rapid City
www.bhsu.edu

## Overview

The BHSU expeience goes beyond the class room. The scenic Black Hills that surround the campus not only offer endless opportunities for recreation, they are also hosts to many unique research opportunities. BHSU offers the best of both worlds: a welcoming small-town atmosphere and easy access to all the activities of a larger town just fifty miles away.

## Current students

Full time undergraduates . 1,520
WUE students . . . . . 628/41%
Freshmen out of state . . . . 35%
Freshmen in housing . . . . 77%
All students in housing . . . 20%
Freshman retention . . . . . 72%
Four-year graduation rate. . 25%
Six-year graduation rate. . . 40%

## Deadline

You can enroll up until the first week of classes, but to get the most aid you should apply by March 1.

## Admissions

Acceptance rate . . . . . . .97%
ACT median range . . . . 18-25
SAT median range. . . 990-1140
Grade-point average. . . . .3.37

## WUE costs

WUE tuition* . . . . . . $12,206
Average R & B. . . . . . $8,200
Mandatory fees . . . . . . . .$0
Other . . . . . . . . . . $4,000
COA . . . . . . . . . . .$24,406

*Out-of-state tuition is less than 150% of in-state tuition

## Required/recommended high school coursework

- English. . . . . . . . 4 years
- Math . . . . . . . . . 3 years
- Social studies. . . 3 years
- Science. . . . . . . . 3 years
- Fine Art. . . . . . . 1 year

# South Dakota

## WUE requirements and procedures

WUE is awarded upon admission. WUE students pay the same as non-WUE out-of-state students which is LESS than 150% of in-state tuition.

## Eligible majors

All majors are open to WUE-eligible students

## Air travel information

Students can fly into Rapid City.

## Transfer information

Transfers with a 2.0 GPA and at least 24 credits will pay the out-of-state tuition, which is lower than 150% of the in-state tuition.

## Contact information

admissions@bhsu.edu

# Dakota State University

Madison, SD (pop. 6,809) 133 miles from Sioux Falls
www.dsu.edu

## Overview

Dakota State University in Madison is an innovative university that has incorporated computer technology into all its academic programs. It is a place where excitement about learning is not just something talked about but something lived every day. Dakota State University's reputation for commitment to computer technology has a long history and is regionally and nationally recognized.

## Current students

Full time undergraduates . 1,330
WUE students . . . . . 191/14%
Freshmen out of state . . . . 40%
Freshmen in housing . . . . 90%
All students in housing . . . 42%
Freshman retention . . . . . 75%
Four-year graduation rate . . 30%
Six-year graduation rate. . . 46%

## Deadline

No firm deadline, but it's best to apply as soon as possible for the most aid.

## Admissions

Acceptance rate . . . . . . . 78%
ACT median range . . . . 19-27
SAT median range. . . 950-1260
Grade-point average. . . . . 3.4

## WUE costs

WUE tuition* . . . . . . $12,278
Average R & B. . . . . . $9,959
Mandatory fees . . . . . . . . $0
Other . . . . . . . . . . . $4,000
COA . . . . . . . . . . . $26,237

*Out-of-state tuition is less than 150% of in-state tuition

## Required/recommended high school coursework

- English . . . . . . . . . 4 years
- Math . . . . . . . . . . 3 years
- Social studies . . . . 3 years
- Science . . . . . . . . . 3 years
- Fine Art . . . . . . . . 1 year

# South Dakota

## WUE requirements and procedures

WUE is awarded upon admission. WUE students pay the same as non-WUE out-of-state students which is LESS than 150% of instate tuition.

## Eligible majors

All majors are open to WUE-eligible students

## Air travel information

Sioux Falls is the closest airport, while Minneapolis and Omaha are the next closest.

## Transfer information

GPA of 2.0 and at least 24 transferable credits. Transfers are eligible for WUE for all majors.

## Contact information

admissions@dsu.edu

The Savvy Guide to the 4-Year WUE Colleges

# Northern State University

Aberdeen, SD (pop. 26,791)
four hours west of Minneapolis, MN
www.northern.edu

## Overview

**Northern State University** has been recognized nationally as one of the best and most affordable institutions in the Midwest. It has also been recognized by students as a place where they can follow their dreams and succeed. Since its inception in 1901, **NSU** has been dedicated to providing a superior education. At **NSU**, you'll be more than just a number. Northern boasts one of the most beautiful campuses in the Midwest. Historic buildings blend with modern facilities, all centered around a park-like campus green. The campus is within walking distance of downtown Aberdeen, so students can easily explore the community of about 26,000 people.

## Current students

Full time undergraduates . 1,033
WUE students . . . . . 125/12%
Freshmen out of state . . . . 29%
Freshmen in housing . . . 100%
All students in housing . . . 39%
Freshman retention . . . . . 68%
Four-year graduation rate . . 38%
Six-year graduation rate . . . 55%

## Deadline

March 1 to get the most aid, but you can apply at any time as long as all the paperwork is complete by the time classes start.

## Admissions

Acceptance rate . . . . . . . 80%
ACT median range . . . . 18-24
SAT median range . . . 800-1150
Grade-point average . . . . . 3.4

## WUE costs

WUE tuition* . . . . . . $12,057
Average R & B . . . . . $10,922
Mandatory fees . . . . . . . . $0
Other . . . . . . . . . . . $4,000
COA . . . . . . . . . . $26,979

*Out-of-state tuition is less than 150% of in-state tuition

# South Dakota

## WUE requirements and procedures

WUE is awarded upon admission. WUE students pay the same as non-WUE out-of-state students which is LESS than 150% of instate tuition.

## Required/recommended high school coursework

- English......... 4 years OR ACT English score of 18
- Math .......... 3 years OR ACT Math score of 20
- Social studies.... 3 years OR ACT score of 17
- Science......... 3 years OR ACT Science score of 17
- Fine Art........ 1 year

## Eligible majors

All majors are open to WUE-eligible students

## Air travel information

A regional airport in Aberdeen offers connections from Minneapolis. Students and families can also fly into Fargo, ND or Sioux Falls, SD and rent a car. Each is about a three-hour drive from Aberdeen.

## Transfer information

Transfers will get the out-of-state rate, which is less than 150% of the in-state tuition.

## Contact information

admissions@northern.edu

### Insights from admissions

*From the personal attention you get, to the great faculty and staff, to a strong sense of community here on campus, Northern State has a lot to offer and gives you opportunities for a successful future. You will belong. Be you. Be us. Be Northern.*

The Savvy Guide to the 4-Year WUE Colleges

# South Dakota School of Mines

Rapid City, SD (pop. 67,956)
www.sdsmt.edu

## Overview

South Dakota School of Mines is a science and engineering research university in Rapid City, at the foot of the beautiful Black Hills. Mount Rushmore, the Badlands National Park and Crazy Horse Memorial are all less than an hour away. Rapid City enjoys a relatively mild climate and offers year-round recreational opportunities, including hiking, bicycling, skiing, snowboarding, fishing, and hunting. Our students benefit from immersive learning experiences including undergraduate research, co-ops/internships, and numerous nationally competitive engineering teams.

## Current students

Full time undergraduates . 2,043
WUE students . . . . . 504/25%
Freshmen out of state . . . .53%
Freshmen in housing . . . 100%
All students in housing . . .60%
Freshman retention . . . . .83%
Four-year graduation rate. . .28%
Six-year graduation rate. . .52%

## Deadline

Rolling admissions for all students. The only deadline is January 1 for scholarships—not for the WUE rate.

## Admissions

Acceptance rate . . . . . . .85%
ACT median range . . . . 24-29
SAT median range. . . . . . NR
Grade-point average. . . . .3.57

## WUE costs

WUE tuition* . . . . . . .$15,600
Average R & B. . . . . . $9,500
Mandatory fees . . . . . . . .$0
Other . . . . . . . . . . . $4,000
COA . . . . . . . . . . . .$29,100

*Out-of-state tuition is less than 150% of in-state tuition

# South Dakota

## Required/recommended high school coursework
- English......... 4 years OR ACT English score of 18............
- Math.......... 3 years OR ACT Math score of 20
- Social studies.... 3 years OR ACT score of 17
- Science......... 3 years OR ACT Science score of 17
- Fine Art........ 1 year

## WUE requirements and procedures
WUE is awarded upon admission.

## Eligible majors
All majors are open to WUE students

## Air travel information
Rapid City Regional Airport is seven miles from campus. Rental Cars or taxis/Uber/Lyft are available.

## Transfer information
Students are eligible for WUE with a GPA of 2.75 and at least 24 credits and proof of college algebra readiness.

## Contact information
admissions@sdsmt.edu

## Insights from admissions

*South Dakota Mines is a small STEM university on the edge of the Black Hills. Our university's approach is about exploring the limits through immersive, hands-on learning. Get a top-tier education without breaking the bank and set yourself up for a future filled with abundant job opportunities in your chosen field. At graduation, 98% of our grads are employed within their field of study, making over $70,000 a year. At South Dakota Mines, we empower you on your educational voyage so you can discover your calling and construct an incredible future.*

The Savvy Guide to the 4-Year WUE Colleges

# South Dakota State University

Brookings, SD (pop. 22,591) 50 miles from Sioux Falls
www.sdstate.edu

## Overview

SDSU is in Brookings, a progressive, friendly community that provides students a safe, comfortable environment. A wide variety of athletic, social, and cultural activities are available on campus and in the community, including the South Dakota Art Museum and **SDSU** athletics. The learning environment at **SDSU** extends beyond the traditional classroom with exceptional hands-on learning opportunities, The Performing Arts Center, Raven Precision Agriculture facility, a new engineering complex, new residence halls, Student Union expansion, and state-of-the-art Wellness Center are recent additions to the excellent facilities at **SDSU**.

## Current students

Full time undergraduates . 7,534
WUE students . . . . . 299/4%
Freshmen out of state . . . . .49%
Freshmen in housing . . . . .94%
All students in housing . . .43%
Freshman retention . . . . .80%
Four-year graduation rate. .30%
Six-year graduation rate. . .59%

## Deadline

Rolling admissions. No application required for WUE rate.

## Admissions

Acceptance rate . . . . . . .88%
ACT median range . . . . 19-25
SAT median range. . . 990-1240
Grade-point average. . . . .3.53

## WUE costs

WUE tuition . . . . . . . .$13,166
Average R & B. . . . . .$10,648
Mandatory fees . . . . . . . .$0
Other . . . . . . . . . . . $4,000
COA . . . . . . . . . . .$27,814

*Out-of-state tuition is less than 150% of in-state tuition

## WUE requirements and procedures

WUE is awarded upon admission. WUE students pay the same as non-WUE out-of-state students which is LESS than 150% of instate tuition.

# South Dakota

## Required/recommended high school coursework
- English......... 4 years OR ACT English score of 18.............
- Math .......... 3 years OR ACT Math score of 20
- Social studies.... 3 years OR ACT score of 17
- Science......... 3 years OR ACT Science score of 17
- Fine Art........ 1 year

## Eligible majors
All majors are open to WUE-eligible students

## Air travel information
A transportation service in Brookings, called Brookings Area Transit Authority, will provide shuttle-type rides with a fee to and from Sioux Falls if scheduled in advance. However, probably more commonly, students use connections the university offers across campus to work out ride shares to and from Sioux Falls; a large portion of SDSU students come from that metro area or areas nearby.

## Transfer information
GPA of 2.0 and 24 hours of transferable credits. Out-of-state tuition is less than 150% of in-state tuition.

## Contact information
sdsu.admissions@sdstate.edu

### Insights from admissions
*SDSU offers a very competitive non-resident tuition rate providing opportunities in value that are oftentimes unmatched by other land grant, doctoral level, Division 1 universities across the United States. In the past we've been included in many college search lists as a top option for non-resident students due to the low cost of education, high-quality academic programs, extraordinary out-of-classroom experiences, and a welcoming and safe campus and community environment.*

The Savvy Guide to the 4-Year WUE Colleges

# University of South Dakota

Vermillion, SD (pop. 10,811) 40 miles from Sioux City, IA
www.usd.edu

## Overview

**The University of South Dakota** is in Vermillion, a university-minded community nestled along the bluffs of the Missouri River in the southeast corner of South Dakota. Committed to excellence in education, research and service, the university is South Dakota's designated liberal arts institution. **The University of South Dakota** offers a broad curriculum in liberal arts and professional programs in seven schools and colleges.

## Current students

Full time undergraduates . 4,500
WUE students . . . . . 160/4%
Freshmen out of state . . . .42%
Freshmen in housing . . . .87%
All students in housing . . .37%
Freshman retention . . . . .82%
Four-year graduation rate. .44%
Six-year graduation rate. . .57%

## Admissions

Acceptance rate . . . . . . .99%
ACT median range . . . . 19-25
SAT median range. . 1050-1260
Grade-point average. . . . . 3.5

## WUE costs

WUE tuition . . . . . . .$13,299
Average R & B. . . . . .$10,590
Mandatory fees . . . . . . $510
Other . . . . . . . . . . . $4,000
COA . . . . . . . . . . .$28,399

### Insights from admissions

*Located in the heart of the Midwest, the University of South Dakota offers an enriching academic experience and a vibrant campus culture at an affordable price. With a wide variety of academic programs, state-of-the-art facilities and a supportive community, USD empowers students to explore their passions and achieve their fullest potential. Whether you're drawn to innovative research opportunities or eager to immerse yourself in dynamic student life, USD is the start to an unforgettable collegiate journey.*

# South Dakota

## Deadline
No firm deadline. Applications are accepted up until the beginning of each semester.

## WUE requirements and procedures
WUE is awarded upon admission. WUE students pay the same as non-WUE out-of-state students which is LESS than 150% of instate tuition.

## Required/recommended high school coursework
- English......... 4 years OR ACT English score of 18
- Math .......... 3 years OR ACT Math score of 20
- Social studies.... 3 years OR ACT score of 17
- Science......... 3 years OR ACT Science score of 17
- Fine Art........ 1 year

## Eligible majors
All majors are open to WUE-eligible students

## Air travel information
Shuttles are available depending on need; otherwise students find transportation on their own.

## Transfer information
Transfers with GPA of 2.0 and 24 credits are eligible for all majors.

## Contact information
admissions@usd.edu

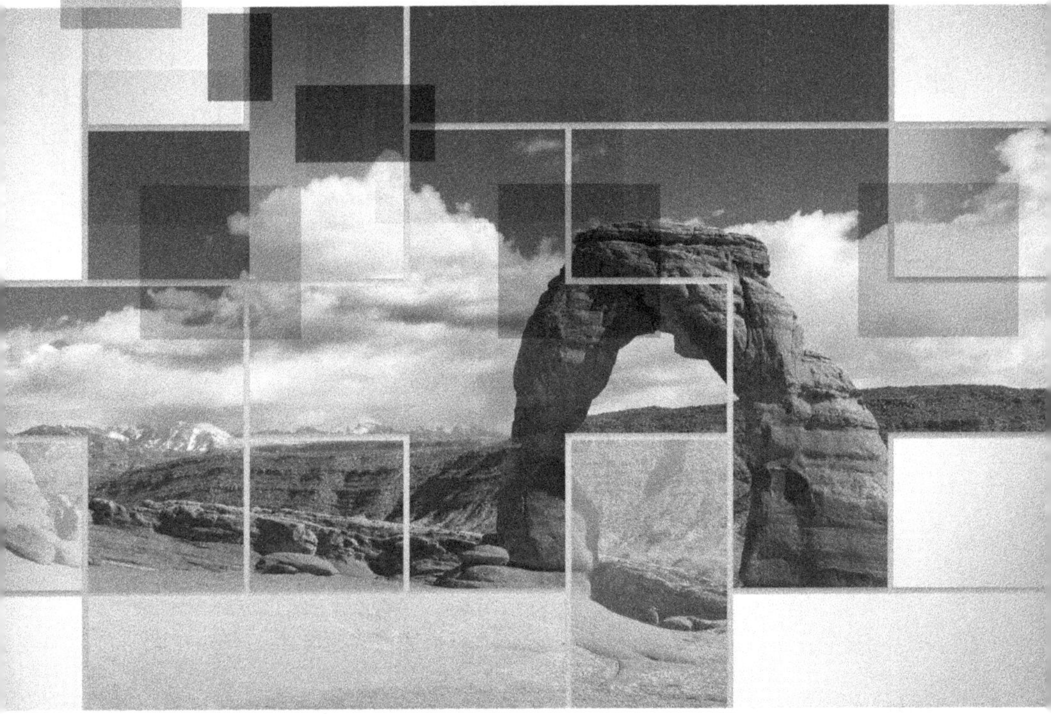

Utah has six four-year WUE colleges. Weber State, Utah Valley University, and Utah State are all large universities with almost 100 percent admission rates. The University of Utah is the state's flagship campus. Southern Utah University serves the southern part of the state and is a medium to small-sized university. Utah Tech is also a medium to small university and serves the southern part of the state. It is an open enrollment university.

# WUE Colleges in utah

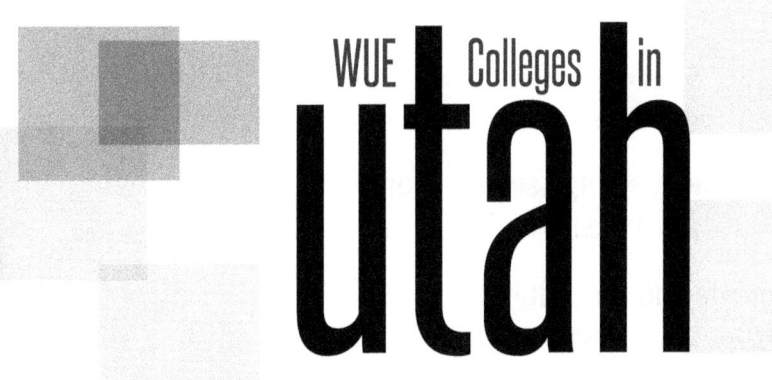

# Southern Utah University

Cedar City, UT (pop. 29,118)
www.suu.edu

## Overview

**Southern Utah University** is committed to providing the most innovative and relevant university experience. **SUU** offers world-class project-based learning, giving students professional experience before they enter the job market. Come learn and play across **SUU**'s hundred acres and beyond, thanks to an educational partnership with the National Park Service alongside SUU Outdoors, which takes students on once-in-a-lifetime adventures. Our safe, residential campus allows students to create lifelong friendships and opportunities to participate in over one hundred sixty clubs and organizations.

## Current students

| | |
|---|---|
| Full time undergraduates | 7,820 |
| WUE students | 450/6% |
| Freshmen out of state | 22% |
| Freshmen in housing | 31% |
| All students in housing | 10% |
| Freshman retention | 71% |
| Four-year graduation rate | 29% |
| Six-year graduation rate | 47% |

## Admissions

| | |
|---|---|
| Acceptance rate | 84% |
| ACT median range | 20-26 |
| SAT median range | 1030-1240 |
| Grade-point average | 3.55 |

## WUE costs

| | |
|---|---|
| WUE tuition | $9,679 |
| Average R & B | $7,788 |
| Mandatory fees | $638 |
| Other | $4,000 |
| COA | $22,105 |

## Deadline

Deadline for the WUE scholarship is the first day of the semester. There is no application fee.

## Required/recommended high school coursework

No classes are required, but the usual high school coursework is suggested.

## WUE requirements and procedures

3.2 GPA OR ACT 24 or SAT 1160.

Utah

### Eligible majors
All majors are open to WUE-eligible students

### Air travel information
Students may take the bus or taxi/Uber/Lyft from the Cedar City airport. Flights from Cedar City only go to and come from Salt Lake City.

### Transfer information
GPA 2.5.

### Contact information
adminfo@suu.edu

### Insights from admissions
*At SUU, it is all about you! You deserve to have an education customized to your goals and dreams. With attentive and engaged faculty that will know your name, the opportunities will be endless on our campus. Plus you are surrounded by the world's best backyard with Zion National Park only 20 minutes from campus.*

### Insights from others
*SUU is well respected in southern Utah and known as providing students with community and opportunities to explore life inside and outside of the classroom. Students enjoy the proximity of national parks and monuments to campus. Undergraduates often speak of the personal attention they receive from their professors.*
  Hailee DeMott
  DeMott College and
    Education Consulting
  Las Vegas, NV

# University of Utah

Salt Lake City, UT (pop. 189,314)
www.utah.edu

## Overview

The **University of Utah** is one of a few WUE colleges that offers a large metropolitan city, skiing and hiking nearby, and Division 1 athletics. **Utah** offers hundreds of areas of academic interests, clubs, and research and internships opportunities.

## Current students

Full time undergraduates  21,189
WUE students . . . . 2318/11%
Freshmen out of state . . . 41%
Freshmen in housing . . . 59%
All students in housing . . 16%
Freshman retention . . . . 85%
Four-year graduation rate . 35%
Six-year graduation rate . . 65%

## Deadline

December 1

## Admissions

Acceptance rate . . . . . . .89%
ACT median range . . . . 22-29
SAT median range. . 1200-1380
Grade-point average. . . . .3.66

## WUE costs

WUE tuition . . . . . . .$15,006
Average R & B. . . . . .$17,442
Mandatory fees . . . . . . . .$0
Other . . . . . . . . . . . $4,000
COA . . . . . . . . . . .$36,448

## Required/recommended high school coursework

- English . . . . . . 4 years  emphasizing composition and literature
- Math . . . . . . . 2 years  beyond elementary algebra (geometry, intermediate algebra. trig, advanced algebra, or calculus).
- History . . . . . . 1 year  American history and government
- Science . . . . . . 3 years  two must be from the following: chemistry, physics, biology or human biology; one of the sciences must include a lab
- Foreign language . 2 years

# Utah

## WUE requirements and procedure
Unweighted GPA of 3.3.

## Eligible majors
All majors are open to WUE-eligible students

## Air travel information
Students must arrange their own travel to the campus..

## Transfer information
3.5 GPA and associates degree or 45 credits.

## Contact information
admissions@utah.edu

### Insights from others
*The University of Utah is the state's public flagship institution and top-tier research university. The campus provides students with many academic and social opportunities every day of the year. For students who desire a large WUE institution, "The U" will provide a true urban college lifestyle with lots of school spirit, Greek life and stunning views of Salt Lake City.*
  *Hailee DeMott*
  *DeMott College and*
    *Education Consulting*
  *Las Vegas, NV*

# Utah State University

Logan, UT (pop. 48,879) 80 miles from Salt Lake City
www.usu.edu

## Overview

Utah State is a thriving research university respected around the world. Students can choose from an array of academic and social opportunities at a university known throughout the world for its intellectual and technological leadership. USU is just minutes from two mountain ranges and within a half-day's drive of six national parks, including Yellowstone and Arches. It provides big-school opportunities with a small-school feel, and all for a great value.

## Current students

Full time undergraduates 17,394
WUE students . . . . . 62 / <1%
Freshmen out of state . . . . .28%
Freshmen in housing . . . . NR
All students in housing . . . NR
Freshman retention . . . . .73%
Four-year graduation rate. .21%
Six-year graduation rate. . .48%

## Deadline

WUE deadline for fall is August 1.

## Admissions

Acceptance rate . . . . . . .89%
ACT median range . . . . 21-28
SAT median range. . . .530-650
Grade-point average. . .520-640

## WUE costs

WUE tuition . . . . . . .$11,745
Average R & B. . . . . .$10,360
Mandatory fees . . . . . . $948
Other . . . . . . . . . . . $4,000
COA . . . . . . . . . . .$27,053

## Required/recommended high school coursework

- English — 4 years
- Math — 4 years
- Social Sciences — 3.5 years
- Science — 3 years (lab-based science, biology, chemistry, physics)
- World Language — 2 years (of same language)

# Utah

## WUE requirements and procedure
Utah State uses a scholarship grid based on GPA and ACT/SAT test scores.
Students with 2.7 GPA and SAT 18/SAT 960 will receive the WUE tuition rate.

## Eligible majors
All majors are open to WUE-eligible students

## Air travel information
The Salt Lake Express goes to and from the airport.

## Transfer information
2.8 GPA.

## Contact information
admit@usu.edu

### Insights from admissions
*Since our founding in 1888, Utah State University has become a premier undergraduate research institution known throughout the world for its intellectual and technological leadership. You graduate with more than a degree; you graduate an Aggie.*

### Insights from others
*Located in Northern Utah, USU is Utah's largest public residential campus. Popular academic programs are mechanical engineering, deaf education, economics, psychology and elementary education. Students enjoy the smaller community of Logan City while experiencing all that a large university provides. Be sure to try their famous Aggie Ice Cream!*
   Hailee DeMott
   DeMott College and Education Consulting
   Las Vegas, NV

# Utah Tech University

St. George, UT (pop. 75,561)
www.utahtech.edu

## Overview

**Utah Tech University,** formerly Dixie State University, offers an education with active learning within all academic disciplines. Hands-on learning, industry partnerships, and a dynamic student-life experience prepare students for successful careers and meaningful lives. All in a location with 300 days of sunshine and a short drive away from several stunning national wonders.

## Current students

| | |
|---|---|
| Full time undergraduates | 5,893 |
| WUE students | 356/6% |
| Freshmen out of state | 26% |
| Freshmen in housing | NR |
| All students in housing | 9% |
| Freshman retention | 56% |
| Four-year graduation rate | 12% |
| Six-year graduation rate | 18% |

## Admissions

| | |
|---|---|
| Acceptance rate | 100% |
| ACT median range | 17-23 |
| SAT median range | 910-1110 |
| Grade-point average | 3.3 |

## WUE costs

| | |
|---|---|
| WUE tuition | $8,352 |
| Average R & B | $7,786 |
| Mandatory fees | $912 |
| Other | $4,000 |
| COA | $21,050 |

## Insights from admissions

*With the lowest tuition of any four-year university in Utah, UTU offers a winning combination of quality education and affordability. Students con come to DSU on the WUE waiver, or they can establish residency after one year and pay around $4,700 per year for resident tuition. Either way, total tuition cost over four years will be roughly $28,000. An excellent value for a four-year degree. The total estimated annual cost is around $21,000. This includes tuition, fees, room and board, transportation and personal expenses.*

# Utah

### Deadline
July 15

### WUE requirements and procedures
2.5 GPA

### Required/recommended high school coursework
None, open enrollment

### Eligible majors
All majors are open to WUE-eligible students

### Air travel information
Students usually fly into Las Vegas. Shuttle bus service is available to the campus. St. George also has a regional airport with taxi service to campus. Uber/Lyft are available as well.

### Transfer information
Must have a 2.75 GPA and 24 credits. All majors are eligible for the WUE.

### Contact information
admissions@dixie.edu

### Insights from others
*Located in conservative St. George, Utah, Utah Tech University is a laid-back campus with many recreational opportunities available to students. Zion National Park is a short 40 mile drive. UTU provides students practical experiences in their majors like internships and clinicals. The size of the student body allows for students to not get lost in the mix and find their community.*
*Hailee DeMott*
*DeMott College and*
*Education Consulting*
*Las Vegas, NV*

The Savvy Guide to the 4-Year WUE Colleges

# Utah Valley University

Orem, UT (pop. 90,749)
about an hour south of Salt Lake City
www.uvu.edu

## Overview

**Utah Valley University** is Utah's largest university. It's an open enrollment university, so anyone can get started with college there. **UVU** has everything a large university would offer, including Division I sports. **UVU** offers many options to get your degree. Although campus supplied housing is not available, WUE students enhance the experience living in the "Residential Engagement Initiative." By living in certain private apartment complexes, the school offer social, educational, service, and recreational programs much like a dorm.

## Current students

Full time undergraduates   17,219
WUE students . . . . .   787/5%
Freshmen out of state . . . . .25%
Freshmen in housing . . . .  0%
All students in housing . . .  0%
Freshman retention . . . . .68%
Four-year graduation rate. . .15%
Six-year graduation rate. . .35%

## Admissions

Acceptance rate . . . . . . 100%
ACT median range . . . . 18-25
SAT median range. . . . . . NR
Grade-point average. . . . .3.45

## WUE costs

WUE tuition . . . . . . . $9,024
Average R & B* . . . . .$10,000
Mandatory fees . . . . . . $658
Other . . . . . . . . . . $4,000
COA . . . . . . . . . .$23,982
(*Off-campus housing)

## Deadline

August 1

## WUE requirements and procedures

2.75 GPA.

## Required/recommended high school coursework

None are required.

# Utah

## Eligible majors
All except global aviation and nursing.

## Air travel information
Shuttle buses run from the Salt Lake City airport to Orem.

## Transfer information
3.0 GPA

## Contact information
admissions@uvu.edu

### Insights from others
*UVU is the largest public university in Utah and is open admissions. Students can choose from over 250 degree options and 150 clubs. Housing can be challenging as students are competing with students at nearby Brigham Young University. Begin your housing search soon!*
*Hailee DeMott*
*DeMott College and Education Consulting*
*Las Vegas, NV*

The Savvy Guide to the 4-Year WUE Colleges

# Weber State University

Ogden, UT (pop. 89,793)
35 miles from Salt Lake City
www.weber.edu

## Overview
Nestled in the foothills of the majestic Wasatch Mountains of northern Utah, **Weber State University** is a one-of-a-kind institution. What makes **WSU** so special is a unique blend of a small-campus feel with big-campus opportunities. The class sizes are small, yet **WSU** offers more than 225 academic programs. The tuition is one of the lowest in the country yet **WSU** offers wonderful faculty and facilities, as well as amazing opportunities for involvement, activities, recreation and so much more..

## Current students
Full time undergraduates   10,103
WUE students . . . . . 91/<1%
Freshmen out of state . . . . 9%
Freshmen in housing . . . .12%
All students in housing . . . 3%
Freshman retention . . . . .66%
Four-year graduation rate. .17%
Six-year graduation rate. . .40%

## Deadline
December 1 priority deadline.

## Admissions
Acceptance rate . . . . . . 100%
ACT median range . . . . 18-25
SAT median range. . . . . . NR
Grade-point average. . . . .3.33

## WUE costs
WUE tuition . . . . . . . $9,368
Average R & B. . . . . .$10,764
Mandatory fees . . . . . . $789
Other . . . . . . . . . . . $4,000
COA . . . . . . . . . . .$24,921

## WUE requirements and procedures
WUE is awarded upon admission.

## Required/recommended high school coursework
High school graduation or equivalent required. No specific high school coursework is required for admission.

Utah

### Eligible majors
All majors are available except dental hygiene or nursing.

### Air travel information
It's about a 40 minute drive from the Salt Lake City airport.

### Transfer information
Must have 30 semester credit hours and all majors are eligible except dental hygiene, nursing, and teacher education. Students with fewer than 30 completed credit hours should apply as a freshman.

### Contact information
admissions@weber.edu

### Insights from admissions
*WSU has several non-resident scholarship options that can be more beneficial than WUE. Depending on your eligibility, our four-year (eight semesters) academic scholarships can cover more of the cost and you can also get an additional tuition incentive for living on campus. Check out all nonresident scholarship options at weber.edu/scholarship.*

### Insights from others
*WSU is located in Ogden, Utah which provides a true mountain-to-metro city living experience. The campus is situated at the base of the Wasatch Mountains so students enjoy outdoor recreation and all four seasons. Weber is all about quality and value and is known for its nursing, radiologic sciences and computing programs..*
*Hailee DeMott*
*DeMott College and Education Consulting*
*Las Vegas, NV*

Washington

The University of Washington is not part of WUE. Central, Eastern, and Western Washington are medium sized WUE colleges. Washington State University is a very large university. Washington State – Tri-cities and Washington State – Vancouver enroll a minimal number of WUE students, so are not included. Evergreen State College is a unique public liberal arts college that is famous for not giving out grades for classes..

# WUE Colleges in Washington

# Central Washington University

Ellensburg, WA (pop. 18,348) 110 miles from Seattle
www.cwu.edu

## Overview

Central's commitment to hands-on learning and discovery and individual attention takes students beyond the limits of the classroom and books. Students get to do what they're studying in real-world, professional settings, which makes learning exciting and relevant. Each year **CWU** graduates thousands of well-educated citizens who are ready for high-demand careers in the workforce. **CWU** prepares students to succeed in a global economy through strong partnerships with thirty colleges and universities around the world.

## Current students

Full time undergraduates . 8,288
WUE students . . . . . 104/1%
Freshmen out of state . . . . 8%
Freshmen in housing . . . .72%
All students in housing . . .28%
Freshman retention . . . . .68%
Four-year graduation rate. .34%
Six-year graduation rate. . .55%

## Deadline

March 1

## Admissions

Acceptance rate . . . . . . .90%
ACT median range . . . . 17-23
SAT median range. . . 920-1090
Grade-point average. . . . . 3.1

## WUE costs

WUE tuition . . . . . . .$11,203
Average R & B. . . . . .$16,814
Mandatory fees . . . . . $2,186
Other . . . . . . . . . . . $4,000
COA . . . . . . . . . . .$34,203

## WUE requirements and procedures

WUE is awarded upon admission.

## Required/recommended high school coursework

- English . . . . . . 4 years
- Math . . . . . . . 3 years   algebra 1, geometry, algebra 2, plus 1 post-

# Washington

algebra 2 class

Acceptable courses include algebra 1, algebra 2, geometry, pre-calculus and above, math analysis, statistics, applied math, appropriate career and technical courses, or an algebra-based science course such as chemistry or physics. If you take and pass pre-calculus, math analysis or calculus prior to your senior year, you're exempt from this requirement.

- Social studies . . . 3 years
- Science . . . . . . 2 years   1 algebra-based lab science
- World language . . 2 years
- Fine/perf. art. . . .1 year   or additional class from other 5 categories

## Eligible majors

All majors are open to WUE-eligible students

## Air travel information

A shuttle that runs from SEA-TAC airport to campus five times per day.

## Transfer information

WUE is awarded upon admission.

## Contact information

admissions@cwu.edu

## Insights from others

*This college has a nice balance of size, not too big, but plenty of majors and opportunities. Theater is really strong here ... really. If you don't mind living surrounded by ranching country, this would be a nice place to live for four years. Great little downtown nearby as a bonus and a major ski area an hour away.*

*Brian Swan*
*Greatland College*
*Consulting*
*Anchorage, AK*

# Eastern Washington University

Cheney, WA (pop. 11,018) sixteen miles from Spokane
www.ewu.edu

## Overview

Eastern Washington University offers students Washington state's best value in higher education. Students can take advantage of the lowest tuition of any four-year public university in the state, yet they have unparalleled opportunity to research alongside their professors. In Cheney, a cozy college town, we're just 20 minutes from Spokane, the state's second-largest city and a major source of internships and career opportunities for our students. There's a reason **Eastern**'s EPIC Adventures program is one of the most popular and well-run outdoor adventure programs in the country: with access to some of country's best adventures. Every weekend students rock climb, ice climb, canoe, kayak, raft, cycle, mountain bike, hike, backpack, camp, swim, ski, mountaineer and more. If it's adventure, and if it's outdoors, you can do it near **EWU**.

## Current students

Full time undergraduates . 5,704
WUE students . . . . . . 48/1%
Freshmen out of state . . . . 8%
Freshmen in housing . . . .68%
All students in housing . . .23%
Freshman retention . . . . .66%
Four-year graduation rate. . .30%
Six-year graduation rate. . .47%

## Deadline

February 1.

## Admissions

Acceptance rate . . . . . . .91%
ACT median range . . . . 19-26
SAT median range. . . . . . NR
Grade-point average. . . . 3.268

## WUE costs

WUE tuition . . . . . . .$11,664
Average R & B. . . . . .$16,116
Mandatory fees . . . . . $1,100
Other . . . . . . . . . . . $4,000
COA . . . . . . . . . . .$32,880

## WUE requirements and procedures

WUE is awarded upon admission.

# Washington

## Required/recommended high school coursework
- English . . . . . . 4 years
- Math . . . . . . . 3 years   algebra 1, geometry, algebra 2
- Social studies . . . 3 years
- Science . . . . . . 2 years   1 algebra-based lab science
- World language . . 2 years
- Fine/perf. art. . . . .1 year   or extra credit from the above core classes
- EWU also has a quantitative requirement, which is a math-based course above algebra: pre-calculus, calculus, chemistry, anatomy and physiology, etc.

## Eligible majors
All majors are open to WUE-eligible students except the last two years of nursing.

## Air travel information
Students must get to campus on their own.

## Transfer information
WUE is awarded upon admission.

## Contact information
admissions@ewu.edu

## Insights from others
*I really like this school, especially for first-generation students. I think they do a good job and put a lot of their resources into students whose families have no background with college and how it all works. A nice size school with lots of majors and activities. But they really shine with advice and support to help you get your degree.*
 Brian Swan
 Greatland College
 Consulting
 Anchorage, AK

# The Evergreen State College

Olympia, WA (pop. 46,479))
www.evergreen.edu

## Overview

**The Evergreen State College** is just outside of Olympia, nestled among emerald Pacific Northwest forests and beaches. Here you'll find a community committed to rigorous academic inquiry, social justice and sustainability. At Evergreen, you can mix a variety of interests and instead of declaring a major, develop your own area of emphasis in more than 40 fields of study based on your unique goals. Paths A Path is a set of programs and courses that provide a way to move from introductory to advanced undergraduate study in one or more related fields. Students at Evergreen can identify with a path developed by the college or design their own to build an area of emphasis.

## Current students

Full time undergraduates . . 1,649
WUE students . . . . . 149/9%
Freshmen out of state . . . . 30%
Freshmen in housing . . . . 62%
All students in housing . . . 15%
Freshman retention . . . . . 65%
Four-year graduation rate. . 31%
Six-year graduation rate. . . 41%

## Deadline

May 1

## Admissions

Acceptance rate . . . . . . . 74%
ACT median range . . . . 22-29
SAT median range. . . 980-1220
Grade-point average. . . . . 3.3

## WUE costs

WUE tuition . . . . . . . $12,541
Average R & B. . . . . . $17,810
Mandatory fees . . . . . $1,248
Other . . . . . . . . . . . $4,000
COA . . . . . . . . . . . $35,599

## WUE requirements and procedures

3.5 GPA unweighted

# Washington

## Required/recommended high school coursework
- English . . . . . 4 credits
- Math . . . . . . 3 credits (algebra 1 and higher)
- Social studies . . 3 credits
- Science . . . . . 2 credits 1 algebra-based lab science
- Foreign language 2 credits (single language)
- Lab science . . 2 credits (1 credit in algebra-based chemistry or physics)
- Art or elective from one are above . . 1 credit

## Eligible majors
All fields of study are available to WUE students.

## Air travel information
Capital Aeroporter shuttle service or Amtrak from Seattle International, along with Uber/Lfyt.

## Transfer information
2.8 GPA.

## Contact information
pedersee@evergreen.edu

### Insights from admissions
*Beginning in with fall 2020 admissions, we have been a test-optional school.*

### Insights from others
*To emulate the real world, students are given performance evaluations instead of grades. Students take about one class a semester that integrates many disciplines taught by teaching teams such as Analyzing Permaculture Systems, which incorporates agriculture, environmental studies, math, and sustainability studies or Almighty God(s) in the Middle East, encompassing history, classics, law/government, political science, and religion.*
  *Brian Swan*
  *Greatland College*
  *Consulting*
  *Anchorage, AK*

# Washington State University

Pullman, WA (pop. 31,395)
www.wsu.edu
Rates as of December 2015

## Overview

WSU is proud of its irrepressible Cougar spirit. Students can find over two hundred fields of study and experience hundreds of hands-on learning opportunities. Students will leave with excellent career preparations from renowned and accessible faculty. At **WSU**, students develop lifelong friendships in a supportive community, all with cutting-edge classrooms and libraries.

## Current students

Full time undergraduates 19,726
WUE students . . . . 1,407/7%
Freshmen out of state . . . . 16%
Freshmen in housing . . . .80%
All students in housing . . .23%
Freshman retention . . . . .80%
Four-year graduation rate. .41%
Six-year graduation rate. . .62%

## Deadline

March 31

## Admissions

Acceptance rate . . . . . . .83%
ACT median range . . . . 20-28
SAT median range. . 1020-1260
Grade-point average. . . . . 3.5

## WUE costs

WUE tuition . . . . . . . .$17,404
Average R & B. . . . . .$18,774
Mandatory fees . . . . . $1,588
Other . . . . . . . . . . . $4,000
COA . . . . . . . . . . . .$41,766

## Required/recommended high school coursework

- English . . . . . . 4 years  3 of composition and literature
- Math . . . . . . . 3 years  algebra 1, geometry, algebra 2 and an additional post-algebra 2 class
- Social studies . . . 3 years
- Science . . . . . . 2 years  1 must be algebra-based
- World language. . 2 years
- Fine art . . . . . . . .1 year  or an additional year of the courses above

# Washington

## WUE requirements and procedures
3.7 GPA, unweighted, will receive a $15,000 scholarship. Cougar Award: 3.0 GPA earns $12,000 scholarship.

## Eligible majors
All majors are open to WUE-eligible students.

## Air travel information
If you are flying into Pullman you have a couple options. The Pullman-Moscow Airport is two miles from campus and you can grab a cab/Uber/Lyft from there. The Lewiston Regional Airport is about 45 minutes away from Pullman in Lewiston, Idaho. Spokane International Airport, which is an hour and a half away from Pullman, is served by most airlines. You can take the Wheatland Express (800-334-2207) from that airport to Pullman for a $38 fee as of 2024.

## Transfer information
3.0 GPA or higher with at least 27 transferable credits

## Contact information
admissions@wsu.edu

### Insights from others
*WSU is great if you're looking for a truly large WUE school. For big-time sports, a great school spirit, and a true "college town" location, you'll have all the opportunities you'd expect from a school like WSU.*
   *Brian Swan*
   *Greatland College Consulting*
   *Anchorage, AK*

### Insights from admissions
*With the WUE Distinguished Cougar Award, an out-of-state student may receive an $11,000 award (2024), renewable for an additional three years. Qualified students receive the award automatically, and are notified upon their offer of admission to WSU. No additional action or forms are required for consideration.*

The Savvy Guide to the 4-Year WUE Colleges

# Western Washington University

Bellingham, WA (pop. 82,234) 55 miles from Vancouver, BC
www.wwu.edu

## Overview

With fifteen thousand students, one hundred sixty academic programs, and an energized campus community, **Western** offers the focus on students and the faculty access of a smaller college and the academic choice, resources, multicultural diversity, and room to grow of a large university. Not so big that you feel like a number; not so small that you have to conform to a mold. Large enough for you to define yourself and small enough that you make a difference.

## Current students

Full time undergraduates 12,247
WUE students . . . . . 384/3%
Freshmen out of state . . . . .16%
Freshmen in housing . . . .85%
All students in housing . . .30%
Freshman retention . . . . .79%
Four-year graduation rate. . .42%
Six-year graduation rate. . .66%

## Deadline

January 31

## Admissions

Acceptance rate . . . . . . .91%
ACT median range . . . . 23-29
SAT median range. . 1120-1340
Grade-point average. . . . . 3.5

## WUE costs

WUE tuition . . . . . . .$12,785
Average R & B. . . . . .$16,107
Mandatory fees . . . . . $1,419
Other . . . . . . . . . . . $4,000
COA . . . . . . . . . . . .$34,311

## Required/recommended high school coursework

- English. . . . . . . . . . . . . . . 4 years
- Math . . . . . . . . . . . . . . . . 3 years  algebra 1, geometry, algebra 2
- Social studies. . . . . . . . . . 3 years
- Science. . . . . . . . . . . . . . . 2 years  1 of algebra-based chemistry or physics; 1 year must include a lab
- World language. . . . . . . . . 2 years
- Fine/performing arts. . . . 1 semester

# Washington

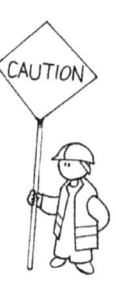

## WUE requirements and procedures

WUE is competitive, based on unweighted GPA, with a minimum GPA of 3.5. Past recipients have a 3.9 GPA and 30 ACT/1400 SAT. In 2023, 384 students were receiving the WUE rate.

## Eligible majors

All majors are open to WUE-eligible students.

## Air travel information

Shuttle service to SEA-TAC airport is available during school breaks. Boltbus, Greyhound, and Amtrak can be used with a transfer to Link Light Rail, which goes to the airport. Students can contact Western Student Transportation for individual help.

## Transfer information

Transfer students are not eligible for WUE.

## Contact information

admit@wwu.edu

### Insights from others

*The WUE is very competitive for this school, which is worth the challenge. It's one of the better academic schools in the program and has the feel of a top-notch research university with the size and access of a smaller mid-sized university. Just sixty miles from Canada, Western gives its students the beauty of the Pacific Northwest along with a quality education. Students are generally serious and hard-working.*
*Brian Swan*
*Greatland College Consulting*
*Anchorage, AK*

Wyoming

Wyoming has one four-year WUE school, the University of Wyoming. It is a medium-sized university and uses a grid based on standardized test scores and GPA to determine WUE eligibility.

# WUE Colleges in
# wyoming

# University of Wyoming

Laramie, WY (pop. 31,814)
www.uwyo.edu

## Overview

Each year the **University of Wyoming** welcomes students from all 50 states and across the globe. With a low student-to-faculty ratio of 15:1, UW is a community of scholars and learners committed to excellence. The **University of Wyoming**'s academic programs of distinction are focused in six broad areas: science and technology, the arts and humanities, environment and natural resources, life sciences, and professions critical to the state and region. The opportunities are endless at the **University of Wyoming**.

## Current students

Full time undergraduates . 7,061
WUE students . . . . . 174/2%
Freshmen out of state . . . . 40%
Freshmen in housing . . . . 82%
All students in housing . . . 26%
Freshman retention . . . . . 75%
Four-year graduation rate. . 39%
Six-year graduation rate. . . 61%

## Admissions

Acceptance rate . . . . . . . 96%
ACT median range . . . . 20-27
SAT median range. . 1030-1230
Grade-point average. . . . . 3.53

## WUE costs

WUE tuition . . . . . . . $8,100
Average R & B. . . . . . $14,000
Mandatory fees . . . . . $2,846
Other . . . . . . . . . . . $4,000
COA . . . . . . . . . . . $28,946

## Deadline

Rolling admissions

## Required/recommended high school coursework

- English . . . . . . 4 years
- Math . . . . . . . 4 years algebra 1, geometry, algebra 2
- Science . . . . . . 4 years    1 of physics or chemistry or college prep physical science
- Social Studies. . . 3 years
- Additional . . . . 4 years (foreign language, performing arts or career vocation education. 2 years must be sequenced in the same discipline.

# Wyoming

## WUE requirements and procedures
3.75 gpa and 27 or 1260 (not superscored)

## Eligible majors
All majors are open to WUE-eligible students.

## Air travel information
Green Ride Colorado shuttle makes stops at the Denver airport, about two hours away, and at the airport in Laramie. The shuttle makes about eight trips per day.

## Transfer information
3.8 GPA.

## Contact information
admissions@uwyo.edu

## Insights from others
*The WUE tuition is difficult to receive, but lots of other merit scholarships are available. Generally outdoorsy Wyoming students here and the cold windy winters are easily dealt with. Nice size: big enough for lots of options, but not huge classes where students feel they are just a number.*
*Brian Swan*
*Greatland College Consulting*
*Anchorage, AK*

The Savvy Guide to the 4-Year WUE Colleges

# The lists

The following pages present data for all the WUE colleges in ranked lists, for easy comparisons. The same data are presented in college-by-college format with the detailed descriptions of individual schools. The explanations that follow also largely duplicate those found at the beginning of the book. This is purely as a matter of convenience for readers, so you won't have to flip back and forth.

## Using The Lists

One thing to remember, and this is important: the data supplied tell only part of each college's story. Numbers do not really tell us the quality of teaching. Data does not tell us the spirit of a university. Metrics do not tell us how intense a discussion might be in a typical political science class or about the passion of a professor of medieval history. They can give us a sense of some aspects of a particular college and that is why I include them in this book. These lists could be useful in finding the school that best fits what you're looking for in your college experience. If tuition is your biggest concern, focus on the low-cost schools. If you want a larger or smaller WUE school, make sure you focus on that part. If you want to be with several others who are also from out of state, take a close look at that metric. In other words, decide what's important to you and use the lists as a guide to help you find your best college fit. Small statistical differences do not matter. A college that has 8 percent of students from out of state is not much different, as far as that particular data point is concerned, than a school that has 12 percent of students from out of state. On the other hand, a school that accepts 100 percent of its applicants is different from a school that accepts only 60 percent of students who apply. A school that has 6 5 percent of its freshman return for their sophomore year is not necessarily better than a school that has 58 percent of its freshmen return. Think of the lists in groupings rather than rankings from one to seventy-eight. For the most important factors to you, look at the top or middle of the list. Whether it be location, size, or housing, you determine what is most important to you.

Bottom line: Decide what you want to get out of your college experience. Use the lists to help you in finding the school that best fits what you're looking for in your college experience.

## Number of full-time undergraduates

I use this factor to tell us the size of the school—not the size of the physical campus itself—but of course they are related. For this book I like to use the number of full-time undergraduate students because I didn't want to count part-time students or graduate students. WUE students must be full-time undergraduates. Every campus will have part-time students. Some will have a lot, such as the University of Alaska, Anchorage; and some will have fewer. Some colleges will have lots of graduate students. When comparing the sizes of the student bodies for this guidebook, it made sense to me for to compare only full-time undergraduate students.

The number of classes the usual full-time student takes varies from campus to campus. Most campuses consider students to be full time when they take at least twelve credits. In some colleges fifteen credits is what most full-time students take, while at others it's sixteen credits. For comparison's sake, I usually used sixteen credits as full time, unless a school specified fifteen credits as what most full-time undergraduates take. For the scope of this book, one credit one way or the other doesn't make a difference.

The size of a college may be an important factor for you. The bigger the campus, the more choices are available, whether it be your major, choices of class times, housing options, or sports. On the other hand, it's easier to "get lost" in a sea of students. It's definitely a different feel between a big campus, a medium-size campus, and a small one. Some students will prefer a small campus, with one dining area and where you can see every building from the quad. Other want a big campus with one hundred-plus buildings and others prefer something in between. As you can see from the list, WUE schools are big, medium and small. Whether you prefer a small or large college, you can use the list to help you narrow down your choices. There is no right or wrong here. Visiting schools, including non-WUE schools of various sizes, will help decide what size you think you may like. How important this factor is to you, is up to . . . *you!*

**Bottom line: The bigger the school, the more opportunities it has for you. But might you prefer a smaller, close-knit community with a better chance to get to know your fellow students and professors?**

## Number of full-time undergraduates, ordered largest to smallest

Arizona State Univerity. . . . . . . . . . . . . . . . . . . . . . .59,832
Colorado State University. . . . . . . . . . . . . . . . . . . . .22,499
Cal Poly Pomona . . . . . . . . . . . . . . . . . . . . . . . . . . . .21,456
University of Uah. . . . . . . . . . . . . . . . . . . . . . . . . . . .21,189
Northern Arizona University. . . . . . . . . . . . . . . . . .20,010
Washington State University . . . . . . . . . . . . . . . . . .19,726
Oregon State University . . . . . . . . . . . . . . . . . . . . . .19,697
University of Nevada - Las Vegas. . . . . . . . . . . . . . .19,523
Utah Valley University . . . . . . . . . . . . . . . . . . . . . . .17,219
University of Nevada - Reno . . . . . . . . . . . . . . . . . .16,951
Utah State University . . . . . . . . . . . . . . . . . . . . . . . .16,561
University of New Mexico . . . . . . . . . . . . . . . . . . . .13,745
Bosie State University . . . . . . . . . . . . . . . . . . . . . . . .13,402
Montana State University. . . . . . . . . . . . . . . . . . . . .12,403
Western Washington University. . . . . . . . . . . . . . . .12,247
Portland State University . . . . . . . . . . . . . . . . . . . . .11,881
University of Hawaii . . . . . . . . . . . . . . . . . . . . . . . . .11,329
Weber State University . . . . . . . . . . . . . . . . . . . . . . .10,103
New Mexico State University. . . . . . . . . . . . . . . . . . .9,322
Metropolitan State University of Denver . . . . . . . . .9,294
North Dakota State University . . . . . . . . . . . . . . . . .8,902
University of Colorado - Denver . . . . . . . . . . . . . . . .8,369
Central Washington University . . . . . . . . . . . . . . . . .8,288
Southern Utah University. . . . . . . . . . . . . . . . . . . . . .7,820
South Dakota State University. . . . . . . . . . . . . . . . . .7,534
University of Colorado - Colorado Springs . . . . . . .7,249
University of Wyoming . . . . . . . . . . . . . . . . . . . . . . . .7,061
University of North Dakota . . . . . . . . . . . . . . . . . . . 6,991
Univerity of Idaho . . . . . . . . . . . . . . . . . . . . . . . . . . . .6,864
Colorado Mesa University . . . . . . . . . . . . . . . . . . . . .6,418
Utah Tech . . . . . . . . . . . . . . . . . . . . . . . . . . . . . . . . . . .5,893
University of Montana . . . . . . . . . . . . . . . . . . . . . . . .5,781
Eastern Washington University . . . . . . . . . . . . . . . . .5,704
University of Northern Colorado . . . . . . . . . . . . . . .5,364
Idaho State University. . . . . . . . . . . . . . . . . . . . . . . . .5,333
Cal Poly Humboldt. . . . . . . . . . . . . . . . . . . . . . . . . . .4,717
University of South Dakota . . . . . . . . . . . . . . . . . . . .4,500
University of Alaska Anchorage . . . . . . . . . . . . . . . .4,351
Fort Lewis College . . . . . . . . . . . . . . . . . . . . . . . . . . .2,795
Colorado State University - Pueblo . . . . . . . . . . . . . .2,589
Western Oregon University. . . . . . . . . . . . . . . . . . . . .2,446
University of Alaska - Fairbanks . . . . . . . . . . . . . . . .2,276
Southern Oregon University. . . . . . . . . . . . . . . . . . . .2,262

## Number of full-time undergraduates, continued

Oregon Tech . . . . . . . . . . . . . . . . . . . . . . . . . . . . . . . .2,103
Nevada State University . . . . . . . . . . . . . . . . . . . . . . .2,087
University of Hawaii - Hilo. . . . . . . . . . . . . . . . . . . . .2,063
South Dakota School of Mines and Technology . . .2,043
Eastern New Mexico University. . . . . . . . . . . . . . . . .1,974
Lewis Clark State College . . . . . . . . . . . . . . . . . . . . .1,888
Montana State Billings. . . . . . . . . . . . . . . . . . . . . . . .1,868
Western New Mexico University . . . . . . . . . . . . . . . .1,851
Minot State University . . . . . . . . . . . . . . . . . . . . . . .1,767
Evergreen State College . . . . . . . . . . . . . . . . . . . . . . .1,649
Montana Tech . . . . . . . . . . . . . . . . . . . . . . . . . . . . .1,622
Western Colorado University. . . . . . . . . . . . . . . . . . .1,579
Valley State University . . . . . . . . . . . . . . . . . . . . . . .1,526
Black Hills State University . . . . . . . . . . . . . . . . . . .1,520
Eastern Oregon University . . . . . . . . . . . . . . . . . . . .1,469
University of Montana Western. . . . . . . . . . . . . . . . .1,424
Dickinson State University. . . . . . . . . . . . . . . . . . . .1,398
Dakota State University . . . . . . . . . . . . . . . . . . . . . .1,330
New Mexico Tech. . . . . . . . . . . . . . . . . . . . . . . . . . .1,093
Adams State University. . . . . . . . . . . . . . . . . . . . . . .1,055
Northern State University. . . . . . . . . . . . . . . . . . . . .1,033
New Mexico Highlands University . . . . . . . . . . . . . .1,016
Montana State University - Northern. . . . . . . . . . . . . 973
Cal Poly Maritime . . . . . . . . . . . . . . . . . . . . . . . . . . . 911
Mayville State University . . . . . . . . . . . . . . . . . . . . . . 560
University of Alaska Southeast . . . . . . . . . . . . . . . . . . 484

## Number and Percentage of WUE students

At some colleges, WUE is very popular and at others it is almost non-existent. This variation is due to many factors. The largest factor, in my opinion, is that the colleges that have the smallest number of WUE students tend to be those that focus on serving students in their local area. Many of these students also commute to school and tend to be less involved in campus events.

Most students attending an out-of-state college want to be with students who are also involved in the total college experience. Including the number of students attending the college who receive the WUE tuition rate, I think, shows how popular the WUE is at that college. A large number or percentage of students who are getting the WUE tells me the process is not difficult and that the college wants to attract out-of-state students with the WUE tuition waver. This information, along with the percentage of out-of-state students, is helpful in the decision-making process. A college with a large percentage of WUE students would be a more attractive option for most families. A college with a very small number of WUE students would be a red flag. It doesn't mean the school is a bad choice or a bad college, but I think there is a reason why that college doesn't have a lot of WUE students. Just knowing that information will help you make a wiser decision in your college choice.

## Percentage of freshmen in on-campus housing and percentage of all students in on-campus housing

Living on campus is a different dynamic than commuting to campus. It's not necessarily better or worse, but is an important factor to many students. Students at colleges change and mature a lot during their time. Freshmen, more often than not, are living on their own for the first time and making more and more decisions on their own. Seniors are past that point in their lives and are looking for full-time jobs, comfortable on their own, and eager to take the next step. For most colleges, a majority of freshmen live on campus; this is sometimes required. As they progress, more and more students live off campus or in campus apartments. For out-of-state students, where and how you will live while away at college is a bigger consideration than for students who live nearby. Unless you have relatives or close friends you'll be living with and commuting to school, housing is an important consideration. Some colleges consider the residential component essential to the college experience at their institutions. Others don't. For most WUE students, this factor is something to consider.

While this guidebook does not get into each school's specific housing and dining options, the percentage of students who are in on-campus housing is included for a few reasons. The greater the percentage, the greater the housing options usually are. This just makes sense. Also, the greater the percentage, the greater a sense of a residential community exists. Commuters can be very involved in campus activities and those who live in dorms might be less involved, but as a general rule, those who live on campus are more involved in campus activities. As out-of-state students, WUE students will be with more students like themselves (meaning from out of state) at schools that have a larger percentage of students from out of state. As with all the other metrics, the quality of your college experience will not be determined solely by whether or not you live on campus, but it is an important consideration. You'll notice a wide range in these listings. Some schools require freshman to live on campus unless they live at home. Four colleges do not offer housing services. I think the percentage of students, especially freshman, that live in on-campus housing is something that should be considered. (Note: Some universities have smaller "satellite" campuses that usually don't have campus-provided housing options. These are designed primarily for students in those cities and the surrounding areas and I have not included them in my data.)

**Bottom line: As an out-of-state student, how important would it be to you to have a significant portion of your peers also living in dorms, especially the first couple of years?**

## Number of WUE students, from highest to lowest

Northern Arizona University ................4,641
University of Hawaii .........................3,262
University of Nevada - Reno ..................2,723
Bosie State University .......................2,542
University of Uah ............................2,318
Colorado State University ....................2,286
Montana State University ....................1,693
Univerity of Idaho ...........................1,679
University of Nevada - Las Vegas .............1,670
Washington State University ..................1,407
Oregon State University ......................1,033
Portland State University ..................... 857
University of Montana ......................... 841
Arizona State Univerity ....................... 792
Utah Valley University ........................ 787
Southern Oregon University .................... 719
Black Hills State University .................. 628
Colorado Mesa University ...................... 625
University of North Dakota .................... 549
Western Oregon University ..................... 532
South Dakota School of Mines and Technology ... 504
Southern Utah University ...................... 450
University of Colorado - Denver ............... 441
University of Northern Colorado ............... 419
University of Hawaii - Hilo ................... 396
University of Colorado - Colorado Springs ..... 389
Western Washington University ................. 384
University of New Mexico ...................... 369
Utah Tech ..................................... 356
North Dakota State University ................. 340
Minot State University ........................ 327
Oregon Tech ................................... 326
South Dakota State University ................. 299
Fort Lewis College ............................ 286
Utah State University ......................... 275
University of Montana Western ................. 274
University of Alaska - Fairbanks .............. 231
Montana State Billings ........................ 226
Cal Poly Humboldt ............................. 201
Montana Tech .................................. 197
Dakota State University ....................... 191
Eastern Oregon University ..................... 189
New Mexico State University ................... 181
University of Wyoming ......................... 174

# Number of WUE students, from highest to lowest, continued

Adams State University . . . . . . . . . . . . . . . . . . . . . . . . . 173
Colorado State University - Pueblo . . . . . . . . . . . . . . . 166
University of South Dakota . . . . . . . . . . . . . . . . . . . . . 160
Eastern New Mexico University . . . . . . . . . . . . . . . . . 152
Evergreen State College . . . . . . . . . . . . . . . . . . . . . . . 149
Valley State University . . . . . . . . . . . . . . . . . . . . . . . . 143
Dickinson State University . . . . . . . . . . . . . . . . . . . . . 142
Idaho State University . . . . . . . . . . . . . . . . . . . . . . . . 141
University of Alaska Anchorage . . . . . . . . . . . . . . . . . 141
Metropolitan State University of Denver . . . . . . . . . 138
Northern State University . . . . . . . . . . . . . . . . . . . . . 125
Lewis Clark State College . . . . . . . . . . . . . . . . . . . . . . 118
Cal Poly Maritime . . . . . . . . . . . . . . . . . . . . . . . . . . . . 118
Central Washington University . . . . . . . . . . . . . . . . . 104
Montana State University - Northern . . . . . . . . . . . . . 93
Weber State University . . . . . . . . . . . . . . . . . . . . . . . . 91
New Mexico Highlands University . . . . . . . . . . . . . . . 90
Nevada State University . . . . . . . . . . . . . . . . . . . . . . . . 62
Mayville State University . . . . . . . . . . . . . . . . . . . . . . . 61
University of Alaska Southeast . . . . . . . . . . . . . . . . . . 58
Western New Mexico University . . . . . . . . . . . . . . . . . 53
Eastern Washington University . . . . . . . . . . . . . . . . . . 48
Western Colorado University . . . . . . . . . . . . . . . . . . . 37
Cal Poly Pomona . . . . . . . . . . . . . . . . . . . . . . . . . . . . . . 36
New Mexico Tech . . . . . . . . . . . . . . . . . . . . . . . . . . . . . 16

## Percentage of WUE students, from highest to lowest

Black Hills State University . . . . . . . . . . . . . . . . . . . . . . . 41
Southern Oregon University . . . . . . . . . . . . . . . . . . . . . 32
University of Hawaii . . . . . . . . . . . . . . . . . . . . . . . . . . . . 29
South Dakota School of Mines and Technology . . . . . 25
Univerity of Idaho . . . . . . . . . . . . . . . . . . . . . . . . . . . . . . 24
Northern Arizona University . . . . . . . . . . . . . . . . . . . . 23
Western Oregon University . . . . . . . . . . . . . . . . . . . . . 22
Bosie State University . . . . . . . . . . . . . . . . . . . . . . . . . . 19
University of Hawaii - Hilo . . . . . . . . . . . . . . . . . . . . . . 19
Minot State University . . . . . . . . . . . . . . . . . . . . . . . . . 19
University of Montana Western . . . . . . . . . . . . . . . . . . 19
University of Nevada - Reno . . . . . . . . . . . . . . . . . . . . . 16
Adams State University . . . . . . . . . . . . . . . . . . . . . . . . . 16
University of Montana . . . . . . . . . . . . . . . . . . . . . . . . . . 15
Oregon Tech . . . . . . . . . . . . . . . . . . . . . . . . . . . . . . . . . . 15
Montana State University . . . . . . . . . . . . . . . . . . . . . . . 14
Dakota State University . . . . . . . . . . . . . . . . . . . . . . . . 14
Eastern Oregon University . . . . . . . . . . . . . . . . . . . . . . 13
Cal Poly Maritime . . . . . . . . . . . . . . . . . . . . . . . . . . . . . 13
Montana State Billings . . . . . . . . . . . . . . . . . . . . . . . . . 12
Montana Tech . . . . . . . . . . . . . . . . . . . . . . . . . . . . . . . . 12
Northern State University . . . . . . . . . . . . . . . . . . . . . . 12
University of Alaska Southeast . . . . . . . . . . . . . . . . . . 12
University of Uah . . . . . . . . . . . . . . . . . . . . . . . . . . . . . . 11
Mayville State University . . . . . . . . . . . . . . . . . . . . . . . 11
Colorado State University . . . . . . . . . . . . . . . . . . . . . . 10
Colorado Mesa University . . . . . . . . . . . . . . . . . . . . . . 10
Fort Lewis College . . . . . . . . . . . . . . . . . . . . . . . . . . . . 10
University of Alaska - Fairbanks . . . . . . . . . . . . . . . . . 10
Dickinson State University . . . . . . . . . . . . . . . . . . . . . 10
Montana State University - Northern . . . . . . . . . . . . . 10
University of Nevada - Las Vegas . . . . . . . . . . . . . . . . . 9
Evergreen State College . . . . . . . . . . . . . . . . . . . . . . . . . 9
Valley State University . . . . . . . . . . . . . . . . . . . . . . . . . . 9
New Mexico Highlands University . . . . . . . . . . . . . . . . 9
University of North Dakota . . . . . . . . . . . . . . . . . . . . . . 8
University of Northern Colorado . . . . . . . . . . . . . . . . . 8
Washington State University . . . . . . . . . . . . . . . . . . . . . 7
Portland State University . . . . . . . . . . . . . . . . . . . . . . . . 7
Southern Utah University . . . . . . . . . . . . . . . . . . . . . . . 6
Utah Tech . . . . . . . . . . . . . . . . . . . . . . . . . . . . . . . . . . . . . 6
Eastern New Mexico University . . . . . . . . . . . . . . . . . . 6
Lewis Clark State College . . . . . . . . . . . . . . . . . . . . . . . 6
Oregon State University . . . . . . . . . . . . . . . . . . . . . . . . . 5

## Percentage of WUE students, from highest to lowest, continued

Utah Valley University .............................. 5
University of Colorado - Denver .................... 5
University of Colorado - Colorado Springs .......... 5
North Dakota State University ..................... 4
South Dakota State University ..................... 4
Cal Poly Humboldt ................................ 4
University of South Dakota ........................ 4
Western Washington University .................... 3
University of New Mexico ......................... 3
Colorado State University - Pueblo ................. 3
Idaho State University ............................ 3
University of Alaska Anchorage .................... 3
Nevada State University ........................... 3
Western New Mexico University .................... 3
Utah State University ............................. 2
New Mexico State University ...................... 2
University of Wyoming ............................ 2
Western Colorado University ...................... 2
New Mexico Tech ................................. 2
Arizona State Univerity ........................... 1
Metropolitan State University of Denver ............ 1
Central Washington University ..................... 1
Weber State University ............................ 1
Eastern Washington University ..................... 1
Cal Poly Pomona ................................. 1

## Percentage of students in on-campus housing, highest to lowest

| | |
|---|---|
| New Mexico Tech | 78 |
| Cal Poly Maritime | 77 |
| Southern Oregon University | 70 |
| Western Colorado University | 66 |
| University of Montana | 63 |
| South Dakota School of Mines and Technology | 50 |
| Adams State University | 49 |
| Fort Lewis College | 49 |
| Univerity of Idaho | 43 |
| South Dakota State University | 43 |
| Dakota State University | 42 |
| Northern Arizona University | 41 |
| Northern State University | 39 |
| Cal Poly Humboldt | 38 |
| Arizona State Univerity | 38 |
| North Dakota State University | 37 |
| University of South Dakota | 37 |
| University of Alaska - Fairbanks | 36 |
| University of Montana Western | 33 |
| University of Northern Colorado | 33 |
| Montana State University | 32 |
| Valley State University | 32 |
| University of Hawaii - Hilo | 31 |
| Western Washington University | 30 |
| Colorado Mesa University | 28 |
| Dickinson State University | 28 |
| Central Washington University | 28 |
| University of Wyoming | 26 |
| University of North Dakota | 24 |
| Colorado State University | 23 |
| Washington State University | 23 |
| University of New Mexico | 23 |
| New Mexico State University | 23 |
| Eastern Washington University | 23 |
| Montana State University - Northern | 22 |
| Oregon Tech | 21 |
| Black Hills State University | 20 |
| University of Hawaii | 20 |
| New Mexico Highlands University | 20 |
| Western Oregon University | 19 |
| University of Colorado - Denver | 19 |
| Bosie State University | 18 |
| University of Nevada - Reno | 18 |
| Oregon State University | 18 |

## Percentage of students in on-campus housing, continued

Colorado State University - Pueblo .............. 18
Minot State University ......................... 16
University of Uah ............................. 16
University of Colorado - Colorado Springs ......... 16
Cal Poly Pomona .............................. 16
Evergreen State College ........................ 15
Eastern Oregon University ...................... 14
Montana Tech ................................ 14
Eastern New Mexico University ................. 12
Idaho State University ......................... 12
Montana State Billings ......................... 10
University of Alaska Southeast ................... 10
Mayville State University ....................... 10
Southern Utah University ...................... 10
Lewis Clark State College ....................... 10
Western New Mexico University ................. 10
Portland State University ........................ 9
Utah Tech ..................................... 9
Nevada State University ......................... 8
University of Nevada - Las Vegas ................. 5
Weber State University .......................... 3
Utah Valley University .......................... 0
Metropolitan State University of Denver ........... 0

University of Alaska Anchorage ................ NR
Utah State University ......................... NR

## Percentage of freshmen in on-campus housing, highest to lowest

South Dakota School of Mines and Technology .... 100
Northern State University ...................... 100
Dickinson State University ..................... 100
Western Colorado University .................... 97
Valley State University ......................... 95
South Dakota State University .................. 94
Cal Poly Maritime .............................. 93
North Dakota State University .................. 93
Dakota State University ........................ 90
Montana State University ....................... 90
Colorado State University ...................... 90
Fort Lewis College ............................. 89
University of North Dakota ..................... 89
New Mexico Tech ............................... 88
Oregon State University ........................ 88
University of South Dakota ..................... 87
Univerity of Idaho ............................. 86
Cal Poly Humboldt ............................. 86
Western Washington University ................. 85
Northern Arizona University ................... 83
University of Wyoming .......................... 82
Washington State University .................... 81
University of Northern Colorado ................ 80
University of Hawaii - Hilo ..................... 80
Black Hills State University .................... 77
Eastern Oregon University ...................... 74
New Mexico Highlands University ............... 73
Southern Oregon University .................... 72
Adams State University ......................... 72
University of Montana Western ................. 72
Central Washington University .................. 72
Arizona State Univerity ........................ 71
Western Oregon University ..................... 70
University of Montana .......................... 68
Colorado Mesa University ...................... 68
Eastern Washington University ................. 68
University of Nevada - Reno .................... 68
Oregon Tech .................................... 66
Bosie State University .......................... 65
Evergreen State College ........................ 62
University of Uah .............................. 59
University of Alaska - Fairbanks ................ 56
New Mexico State University ................... 56
University of Colorado - Colorado Springs ....... 54

## Percentage of freshmen in on-campus housing, continued

Minot State University .......................... 53
Montana Tech .................................. 51
University of New Mexico ....................... 50
Portland State University ....................... 50
University of Hawaii ........................... 48
Colorado State University - Pueblo ............... 45
Eastern New Mexico University .................. 44
Cal Poly Pomona ............................... 41
Western New Mexico University ................. 40
Montana State University - Northern ............. 39
Montana State Billings ......................... 33
Southern Utah University ....................... 31
University of Colorado - Denver ................. 30
Idaho State University ......................... 25
University of Alaska Southeast .................. 20
Lewis Clark State College ....................... 19
University of Nevada - Las Vegas ................ 18
Weber State University ......................... 12
Mayville State University ....................... 11
Utah Valley University ........................... 0
Metropolitan State University of Denver ........... 0

Nevada State University ....................... NR
University of Alaska Anchorage ................ NR
Utah State University ......................... NR
Utah Tech .................................... NR

## Freshman acceptance rates

One of the sad things in college admissions today is the race to see which schools can accept the lowest percentage of students who apply. Lately Harvard and Stanford have been neck and neck in turning away over 92 percent of the very qualified applicants they receive each year. Many students and families think that if there is so much demand for a particular school that they have to turn so many away, it must be a "good" school. The U.S. News and World Report rankings and the schools themselves have helped fuel this demand. As the percentages of accepted students get lower, the thought is that the quality of the students gets higher. There's a lot of debate about this in general that I will not discuss here, but the data is useful information for WUE school applicants. Every WUE school except one, New Mexico Tech, accepts over half the students that apply. Most accept two-thirds to three-fourths of applicants. Many accept 80-90 percent and some are open enrollment and accept 100 percent. Yes, there is college for everyone. I have included the data so students and families will have an idea of their chances of acceptance, not as a tool to see which of the schools is better.

**Bottom line: Use the acceptance rate to help gauge your chances of acceptance.**

## Percentage of freshmen from out of state

All WUE students are, by definition, out-of-state students. All campuses have out-of-state students, but the number or percentage can vary immensely. Many WUE schools have fewer than 2 percent of their students from out of state. This does not make them better or worse, but from my experience, it does give the student body and campus a different feel. Now for many western states, in-state students may live very far from campus. They may be from a large city, small town, or a farming community. But generally, the higher percentage of in-state students means that they live "nearby." They may be a diverse group of students, but not geographically diverse. They can more easily go home for a weekend. They know the city and the area pretty well. Out-of-state students find going home or visiting friends is much more difficult in comparison. They also don't know the area as well. Where to go for a day hike? The best place to see a show? While figuring out these things can be fun and part of the college experience, it is different when you are two out of a hundred from out of state. It's just a different vibe. The transportation to and from campus is usually more "on your own" at a school with fewer out-of-state students. A school with 20 to 30 percent of its students from out of state will have more geographic diversity. You may meet people from all over the United States. You'll notice that three-fourths of the colleges have at least ten percent from out of state, while the bottom of the list have very few from out of state. How important is this? Each student is different and each can decide how important that factor is. I have included it in the guidebook because I think it is something that should be considered.

Bottom line: Would you prefer to be one of the few out-of-state students or be in a school with a larger population from outside the state?

## Acceptance rate, from lowest to highest

Cal Poly Pomona ................................ 55
Colorado Mesa University ....................... 63
University of Alaska Southeast .................. 63
Montana State University - Northern.............. 64
University of Montana Western................... 70
University of Alaska - Fairbanks ................. 70
University of Colorado - Denver ................. 72
Dickinson State University...................... 72
University of Hawaii ........................... 73
Montana State University....................... 73
Evergreen State College ........................ 74
New Mexico Tech............................... 75
Cal Poly Maritime ............................. 76
Nevada State University ........................ 76
New Mexico State University.................... 78
Dakota State University ........................ 78
Univerity of Idaho ............................. 79
University of New Mexico ...................... 79
Northern State University....................... 80
University of Hawaii - Hilo...................... 80
Colorado State University....................... 81
Northern Arizona University.................... 82
University of Alaska Anchorage ................. 82
Oregon State University ........................ 83
University of North Dakota ..................... 83
Washington State University .................... 83
Oregon Tech .................................. 83
Cal Poly Humboldt............................. 83
University of Nevada - Las Vegas................. 83
Bosie State University ......................... 84
Southern Utah University....................... 84
South Dakota School of Mines and Technology ..... 85
University of Northern Colorado ................ 85
Valley State University ........................ 85
University of Colorado - Colorado Springs ......... 85
University of Nevada - Reno .................... 86
South Dakota State University................... 88
University of Uah.............................. 89
Montana Tech ................................ 89
Arizona State Univerity........................ 90
Central Washington University .................. 90
Western Washington University................. 91
Western Colorado University.................... 91
Eastern Washington University ................. 91

224

## Acceptance rate, from lowest to highest, continued

Minot State University ........................... 93
Fort Lewis College .............................. 93
Western Oregon University....................... 93
Utah State University ........................... 94
Southern Oregon University...................... 94
Eastern New Mexico University................... 95
North Dakota State University ................... 95
University of Montana ........................... 95
New Mexico Highlands University ................ 95
Mayville State University ........................ 95
University of Wyoming........................... 96
Black Hills State University ...................... 97
Portland State University ........................ 98
Metropolitan State University of Denver ........... 98
University of South Dakota ...................... 99
Colorado State University - Pueblo ................ 99
Eastern Oregon University ....................... 99
Idaho State University........................... 99
Adams State University.......................... 99
Western New Mexico University ................. 99
Weber State University ......................... 100
Utah Valley University ......................... 100
Lewis Clark State College ....................... 100
Montana State Billings.......................... 100
Utah Tech ..................................... 100

The Savvy Guide to the 4-Year WUE Colleges

## Percentage of freshmen from out of state, from highest to lowest

North Dakota State University .................... 65
Montana State University ........................ 62
University of North Dakota ....................... 62
Fort Lewis College .............................. 60
South Dakota School of Mines and Technology ..... 53
South Dakota State University .................... 49
University of Montana ........................... 47
University of Hawaii ............................ 46
Bosie State University .......................... 42
University of South Dakota ...................... 42
Oregon State University ......................... 41
University of Uah .............................. 41
Dakota State University ......................... 40
Colorado State University ....................... 40
University of Wyoming ........................... 40
Southern Oregon University ...................... 39
Adams State University .......................... 39
Arizona State Univerity ......................... 38
Dickinson State University ...................... 37
Valley State University ......................... 37
Western Oregon University ....................... 37
Black Hills State University .................... 35
University of Hawaii - Hilo ..................... 31
Oregon Tech .................................... 31
Eastern Oregon University ....................... 31
Evergreen State College ......................... 30
Univerity of Idaho .............................. 30
Mayville State University ....................... 30
Western New Mexico University ................... 30
Northern State University ....................... 29
Western Colorado University ..................... 28
Minot State University .......................... 28
Utah State University ........................... 28
Northern Arizona University ..................... 27
New Mexico State University ..................... 26
Utah Tech ...................................... 26
University of Montana Western ................... 25
Utah Valley University .......................... 25
University of Nevada - Reno ..................... 24
Eastern New Mexico University ................... 23
Portland State University ....................... 23
Southern Utah University ........................ 22
Lewis Clark State College ....................... 22

## Percentage of freshmen from out of state, continued

University of New Mexico . . . . . . . . . . . . . . . . . . . . . . . 21
Montana Tech . . . . . . . . . . . . . . . . . . . . . . . . . . . . . . . . 21
Colorado State University - Pueblo . . . . . . . . . . . . . . . . 21
Montana State University - Northern . . . . . . . . . . . . . 20
University of Colorado - Colorado Springs . . . . . . . . . 20
University of Alaska - Fairbanks . . . . . . . . . . . . . . . . . . 18
University of Colorado - Denver . . . . . . . . . . . . . . . . . 18
Colorado Mesa University . . . . . . . . . . . . . . . . . . . . . . . 17
University of Northern Colorado . . . . . . . . . . . . . . . . . 17
New Mexico Highlands University . . . . . . . . . . . . . . . . 17
Cal Poly Maritime . . . . . . . . . . . . . . . . . . . . . . . . . . . . . 16
Washington State University . . . . . . . . . . . . . . . . . . . . 16
Western Washington University . . . . . . . . . . . . . . . . . 16
University of Nevada - Las Vegas . . . . . . . . . . . . . . . . . 14
Idaho State University . . . . . . . . . . . . . . . . . . . . . . . . . 11
Montana State Billings . . . . . . . . . . . . . . . . . . . . . . . . . 11
New Mexico Tech . . . . . . . . . . . . . . . . . . . . . . . . . . . . . 10
Weber State University . . . . . . . . . . . . . . . . . . . . . . . . . . 9
University of Alaska Southeast . . . . . . . . . . . . . . . . . . . . 8
Central Washington University . . . . . . . . . . . . . . . . . . . 8
Eastern Washington University . . . . . . . . . . . . . . . . . . . 8
University of Alaska Anchorage . . . . . . . . . . . . . . . . . . . 7
Cal Poly Humboldt . . . . . . . . . . . . . . . . . . . . . . . . . . . . . 7
Metropolitan State University of Denver . . . . . . . . . . . 5
Nevada State University . . . . . . . . . . . . . . . . . . . . . . . . . 2
Cal Poly Pomona . . . . . . . . . . . . . . . . . . . . . . . . . . . . . . . 1

## Percentage freshman retention

The freshman retention rate is what percentage of freshmen return for their second or sophomore year. One might think that the higher the rate, the better the school, but I think it tells more about the type of student and about the students' willingness to return. Let me explain. If you look at the schools with the highest freshman retention rates, it usually mirrors the schools with the lowest acceptance rates. Why? Well, those who get accepted into a "top" university are the type of students who are likely to return for their sophomore year. If you took the same pool of students and they went to other schools as freshman, they would be highly likely to return to those schools as well. Some schools with lower retention rates have freshmen who might be "seeing if college is for them."

Some other reasons for lower rates are financial. Students may take off after their freshman year to earn more income. They may also decide that college is not for them. They may have been marginal students who didn't really want to go to college, but thought it was "the thing to do." They might have discovered that the school they chose was not the right fit for them. They might start at a local or lower-cost school and then transfer to the school they prefer after having a year under their belt to figure out what they really want to major in.

As you can see, there are many reasons freshmen do not return for their second year. The freshman retention rate tells more about the types of students and their situations than the quality of the education offered. Having said that, I think most people would want to go to a school where most of the students—and the friends they make—will be back for their second year. That's why I included the freshman retention rate and why it can be a useful tool to help you consider the school you want to go to.

**Bottom line:** How important is it to you to know that most of the freshman who start out at your college return for their sophomore year?

## Percentage of freshman retention, from highest to lowest

Oregon State University . . . . . . . . . . . . . . . . . . . . . . . . . 87
Cal Poly Pomona . . . . . . . . . . . . . . . . . . . . . . . . . . . . . . 87
Colorado State University. . . . . . . . . . . . . . . . . . . . . . . . 86
University of Uah. . . . . . . . . . . . . . . . . . . . . . . . . . . . . . . 85
Arizona State Univerity. . . . . . . . . . . . . . . . . . . . . . . . . . 85
South Dakota School of Mines and Technology . . . . . 83
University of South Dakota . . . . . . . . . . . . . . . . . . . . . . 82
South Dakota State University. . . . . . . . . . . . . . . . . . . . 80
Washington State University . . . . . . . . . . . . . . . . . . . . . 80
University of North Dakota . . . . . . . . . . . . . . . . . . . . . . 79
University of Hawaii . . . . . . . . . . . . . . . . . . . . . . . . . . . 79
Bosie State University . . . . . . . . . . . . . . . . . . . . . . . . . . 79
University of Nevada - Reno . . . . . . . . . . . . . . . . . . . . 79
Western Washington University. . . . . . . . . . . . . . . . . . 79
Cal Poly Maritime . . . . . . . . . . . . . . . . . . . . . . . . . . . . . 78
University of Nevada - Las Vegas. . . . . . . . . . . . . . . . . 77
Western Colorado University. . . . . . . . . . . . . . . . . . . . 76
Northern Arizona University. . . . . . . . . . . . . . . . . . . . . 76
Colorado Mesa University . . . . . . . . . . . . . . . . . . . . . . 76
Cal Poly Humboldt. . . . . . . . . . . . . . . . . . . . . . . . . . . . . 76
Nevada State University . . . . . . . . . . . . . . . . . . . . . . . . 76
North Dakota State University . . . . . . . . . . . . . . . . . . 75
Montana State University. . . . . . . . . . . . . . . . . . . . . . . 75
Dakota State University . . . . . . . . . . . . . . . . . . . . . . . . 75
University of Wyoming . . . . . . . . . . . . . . . . . . . . . . . . 75
Univerity of Idaho . . . . . . . . . . . . . . . . . . . . . . . . . . . . . 75
Utah State University . . . . . . . . . . . . . . . . . . . . . . . . . . 75
Montana Tech . . . . . . . . . . . . . . . . . . . . . . . . . . . . . . . . 75
University of Northern Colorado . . . . . . . . . . . . . . . . 75
New Mexico Tech. . . . . . . . . . . . . . . . . . . . . . . . . . . . . . 75
University of Montana . . . . . . . . . . . . . . . . . . . . . . . . . 74
New Mexico State University. . . . . . . . . . . . . . . . . . . . 73
Portland State University . . . . . . . . . . . . . . . . . . . . . . . 73
University of Colorado - Denver . . . . . . . . . . . . . . . . . 73
Black Hills State University . . . . . . . . . . . . . . . . . . . . . 72
Oregon Tech . . . . . . . . . . . . . . . . . . . . . . . . . . . . . . . . . 72
University of New Mexico . . . . . . . . . . . . . . . . . . . . . . 72
University of Alaska - Fairbanks . . . . . . . . . . . . . . . . . 72
Dickinson State University. . . . . . . . . . . . . . . . . . . . . . 71
Western New Mexico University . . . . . . . . . . . . . . . . . 71
University of Montana Western. . . . . . . . . . . . . . . . . . 71
Southern Utah University. . . . . . . . . . . . . . . . . . . . . . . 71
Idaho State University. . . . . . . . . . . . . . . . . . . . . . . . . . 71
Valley State University . . . . . . . . . . . . . . . . . . . . . . . . . 70

## Percentage of freshman retention, continued

University of Hawaii - Hilo ........................ 70
Minot State University ........................... 70
Montana State University - Northern .............. 70
University of Alaska Anchorage ................... 69
Eastern Oregon University ........................ 68
Northern State University ........................ 68
Utah Valley University ........................... 68
Central Washington University .................... 68
University of Colorado - Colorado Springs ......... 67
Southern Oregon University ....................... 66
Weber State University ........................... 66
Eastern Washington University .................... 66
Western Oregon University ........................ 65
Evergreen State College .......................... 65
Fort Lewis College ............................... 63
Lewis Clark State College ........................ 63
Colorado State University - Pueblo ................ 63
University of Alaska Southeast ................... 63
Metropolitan State University of Denver ........... 63
Mayville State University ........................ 61
Montana State Billings ........................... 60
Eastern New Mexico University .................... 59
Utah Tech ........................................ 56
Adams State University ........................... 54

New Mexico Highlands University ................ NR

## Four-year and six-year graduation rates

Four-year and six-year graduation rates tell us what percentage of students graduate in four years and what percentage of students graduate in six years. This is the least reliable data I've included. How to arrive at these numbers can be complicated. If students transfer because they've decided to switch majors and their current school doesn't have their desired major, do they count as students who didn't graduate in four years or six years? A student who stays out of college for a year to earn money and then returns: how is this calculated in the percentage? One would think that the higher the rate, the better the school, but like the freshman retention rate, this piece of data tells us more about the students in general than the school's ability to help their students graduate in four years. Ideally, most students would like to go to school full time for four years and get a degree. Statistically, less than one fourth of college students complete their degree in four years.

In my opinion, the four-year residential college experience is more of a "Hollywoodized" version of college. It often takes more than four years because of the students' various situations. It's usually not the failure of the college to graduate their students in four years. Many of the reasons why students don't return for their second year are also reasons why students don't graduate in four years. Attending part time, switching majors, taking a year off are the most common reasons. Others are transferring schools or changing your mind about what you want in your college experience. As far as college is concerned, it is not unusual for eighteen- or nineteen-year-olds to figure out what they want out of their college experience as they go. How many adults are still figuring out "what to do?" Most students who graduate in four years have a pretty clear plan and the resources—money—to so. So, this tells us more about the students who attend the college than about the college itself.

The schools with the highest four-year and six-year graduation rates have the types of students who are usually high achieving and driven and have the resources to graduate in four or six years. A school with a very low four-year graduation rate has a lot more students who are attending part time or taking a class or two to see if college is for them, and students taking longer for financial reasons. None of these factors reflect on the quality of education. You'll notice from the lists that the six-year graduation rates are much higher than the four-year graduation rates. WUE colleges tend to serve students who don't take the traditional "Hollywoodized" version of college. I still find it a useful tool, though, because it does say something about the students. It might be a one of the factors for WUE students to consider.

**Bottom line: How important is it to you to journey together as a class of freshmen and to graduate in four years?**

## Four-year graduation rate, from highest to lowest

Cal Poly Maritime .................................. 58
Colorado State University ......................... 48
University of North Dakota ........................ 47
Oregon State University ........................... 46
University of Montana Western .................... 45
University of South Dakota ........................ 44
Northern Arizona University ...................... 43
North Dakota State University .................... 43
Western Washington University ................... 42
Arizona State Univerity ........................... 41
South Dakota State University .................... 41
Washington State University ...................... 41
University of Hawaii .............................. 40
University of Nevada - Reno ...................... 40
University of Wyoming ............................ 39
New Mexico Tech .................................. 38
Northern State University ........................ 38
University of Uah ................................. 35
Western Colorado University ..................... 34
Univerity of Idaho ................................ 34
Central Washington University ................... 34
Southern Oregon University ...................... 34
University of New Mexico ........................ 33
Montana State University ........................ 31
University of Colorado - Colorado Springs ......... 31
Evergreen State College .......................... 31
Bosie State University ............................ 30
Dakota State University .......................... 30
Montana Tech .................................... 30
Oregon Tech ..................................... 30
Eastern Washington University ................... 30
Portland State University ........................ 29
Southern Utah University ........................ 29
Cal Poly Pomona ................................. 28
South Dakota School of Mines and Technology ..... 28
Cal Poly Humboldt ............................... 28
Valley State University ........................... 28
Eastern Oregon University ....................... 28
Western Oregon University ...................... 28
Utah State University ............................ 27
Fort Lewis College ............................... 27
Adams State University .......................... 26
Black Hills State University ...................... 25
New Mexico Highlands University ................ 24

## Four-year graduation rate, continued

| | |
|---|---|
| University of Northern Colorado | 24 |
| Montana State University - Northern | 24 |
| University of Montana | 23 |
| New Mexico State University | 23 |
| Minot State University | 23 |
| University of Alaska Anchorage | 22 |
| Lewis Clark State College | 22 |
| University of Hawaii - Hilo | 21 |
| Colorado State University - Pueblo | 21 |
| Eastern New Mexico University | 21 |
| University of Alaska - Fairbanks | 21 |
| University of Colorado - Denver | 20 |
| Idaho State University | 20 |
| Colorado Mesa University | 19 |
| Dickinson State University | 19 |
| Western New Mexico University | 19 |
| University of Nevada - Las Vegas | 18 |
| Weber State University | 17 |
| Mayville State University | 17 |
| Metropolitan State University of Denver | 16 |
| Utah Valley University | 15 |
| Utah Tech | 12 |
| Montana State Billings | 11 |
| University of Alaska Southeast | 10 |
| Nevada State University | 9 |

The Savvy Guide to the 4-Year WUE Colleges

## Six-year graduation rate, from highest to lowest

Oregon State University . . . . . . . . . . . . . . . . . . . . . . . . . 70
Cal Poly Pomona . . . . . . . . . . . . . . . . . . . . . . . . . . . . . . 69
Cal Poly Maritime . . . . . . . . . . . . . . . . . . . . . . . . . . . . . 68
Arizona State Univerity . . . . . . . . . . . . . . . . . . . . . . . . . 68
Colorado State University . . . . . . . . . . . . . . . . . . . . . . . 67
Western Washington University . . . . . . . . . . . . . . . . . . 66
University of Uah . . . . . . . . . . . . . . . . . . . . . . . . . . . . . . 65
University of North Dakota . . . . . . . . . . . . . . . . . . . . . . 63
North Dakota State University . . . . . . . . . . . . . . . . . . . 63
University of Nevada - Reno . . . . . . . . . . . . . . . . . . . . . 63
Washington State University . . . . . . . . . . . . . . . . . . . . 62
University of Hawaii . . . . . . . . . . . . . . . . . . . . . . . . . . . 62
University of Wyoming . . . . . . . . . . . . . . . . . . . . . . . . . 61
Univerity of Idaho . . . . . . . . . . . . . . . . . . . . . . . . . . . . . 60
Bosie State University . . . . . . . . . . . . . . . . . . . . . . . . . . 60
Northern Arizona University . . . . . . . . . . . . . . . . . . . . 59
South Dakota State University . . . . . . . . . . . . . . . . . . . 59
University of South Dakota . . . . . . . . . . . . . . . . . . . . . 57
Montana State University . . . . . . . . . . . . . . . . . . . . . . . 57
Montana Tech . . . . . . . . . . . . . . . . . . . . . . . . . . . . . . . . 57
Oregon Tech . . . . . . . . . . . . . . . . . . . . . . . . . . . . . . . . . 57
Northern State University . . . . . . . . . . . . . . . . . . . . . . 55
Central Washington University . . . . . . . . . . . . . . . . . . 55
Portland State University . . . . . . . . . . . . . . . . . . . . . . . 54
South Dakota School of Mines and Technology . . . . . 52
Utah State University . . . . . . . . . . . . . . . . . . . . . . . . . . 52
University of Northern Colorado . . . . . . . . . . . . . . . . . 52
New Mexico State University . . . . . . . . . . . . . . . . . . . . 51
New Mexico Tech . . . . . . . . . . . . . . . . . . . . . . . . . . . . . 50
University of New Mexico . . . . . . . . . . . . . . . . . . . . . . 50
University of Montana Western . . . . . . . . . . . . . . . . . . 49
University of Colorado - Denver . . . . . . . . . . . . . . . . . 48
Western Colorado University . . . . . . . . . . . . . . . . . . . 47
Eastern Washington University . . . . . . . . . . . . . . . . . . 47
Southern Utah University . . . . . . . . . . . . . . . . . . . . . . 47
Cal Poly Humboldt . . . . . . . . . . . . . . . . . . . . . . . . . . . . 47
University of Montana . . . . . . . . . . . . . . . . . . . . . . . . . 47
University of Nevada - Las Vegas . . . . . . . . . . . . . . . . 47
Southern Oregon University . . . . . . . . . . . . . . . . . . . . 46
Dakota State University . . . . . . . . . . . . . . . . . . . . . . . . 46
Minot State University . . . . . . . . . . . . . . . . . . . . . . . . . 46
Colorado Mesa University . . . . . . . . . . . . . . . . . . . . . . 45
Valley State University . . . . . . . . . . . . . . . . . . . . . . . . . 44
University of Colorado - Colorado Springs . . . . . . . . . 43

## Six-year graduation rate, continued

Fort Lewis College .............................. 43
Montana State University - Northern ............. 42
University of Hawaii - Hilo ...................... 42
Evergreen State College ......................... 41
Western Oregon University ....................... 41
New Mexico Highlands University ................ 41
Black Hills State University ..................... 40
Weber State University .......................... 40
Colorado State University - Pueblo ................ 39
Dickinson State University ...................... 39
Eastern Oregon University ....................... 38
Idaho State University .......................... 36
Mayville State University ....................... 35
Utah Valley University .......................... 35
Eastern New Mexico University .................. 34
Adams State University ......................... 33
University of Alaska - Fairbanks .................. 33
University of Alaska Anchorage .................. 32
Lewis Clark State College ....................... 32
Western New Mexico University .................. 29
Metropolitan State University of Denver .......... 29
Nevada State University ......................... 28
Montana State Billings .......................... 25
University of Alaska Southeast ................... 19
Utah Tech ....................................... 18

## WUE tuition and mandatory fees

While it might be said that tuition is 150 percent of the in-state rate, it can get little more complicated than that. WUE is offered only to full time students. Online and part-time students are not eligible for the WUE tuition. Most colleges consider full-time students to be those taking at least twelve credits per semester. Most full-time students actually take fifteen or sixteen credits, depending on the institution. Some schools charge per credit, while other have a flat rate for "full-time" students. For comparison between schools, I used sixteen credits as the standard, unless most students took fifteen. For the scope of this book, the cost difference and practical use for this variation is minimal. Some schools have out-of-state rates that are less than 150 percent of the in-state rate. In those cases, I just used the out-of-state rate.

This list includes the tuition and mandatory fees added together. Other types of aid are available from all colleges. Aid based on merit or need might make the final cost of attending college less than than the WUE tuition rate. And completing the FAFSA, applying early in the process, and pursuing scholarships—especially those specific to the school to which you are applying—may help you more than the WUE program.

NOTE: The following figures are for the 2023-24 school year. Future rates historically rise 3-5% each year.

# The lists

## Annual tuition and fees, from lowest to highest

Eastern New Mexico University . . . . . . . . . . . . . . . .9,054
Minot State University . . . . . . . . . . . . . . . . . . . . . . .9,192
Utah Tech . . . . . . . . . . . . . . . . . . . . . . . . . . . . . . . . . .9.264
Utah Valley University . . . . . . . . . . . . . . . . . . . . . . .9,682
Western New Mexico University . . . . . . . . . . . . . . .9,820
University of Montana Western . . . . . . . . . . . . . . . .9,877
Dickinson State University . . . . . . . . . . . . . . . . . . . .9,936
Weber State University . . . . . . . . . . . . . . . . . . . . . .10,157
Montana State University- Northern . . . . . . . . . . .10,270
Southern Utah University . . . . . . . . . . . . . . . . . . . .10,317
Montana State University - Billings . . . . . . . . . . . .10,480
Mayville State University . . . . . . . . . . . . . . . . . . . .10,616
Valley City State University . . . . . . . . . . . . . . . . . .10,756
New Mexico Highlands University . . . . . . . . . . . . .10,920
University of Wyoming . . . . . . . . . . . . . . . . . . . . . .10,946
Nevada State University . . . . . . . . . . . . . . . . . . . . .10,972
Lewis-Clark State College . . . . . . . . . . . . . . . . . . . .10,984
Cal Poly Pomona . . . . . . . . . . . . . . . . . . . . . . . . . . .11,375
University of New Mexico . . . . . . . . . . . . . . . . . . .11,445
New Mexico State University . . . . . . . . . . . . . . . . .11,868
Cal Poly Maritime . . . . . . . . . . . . . . . . . . . . . . . . . .11,888
Cal Poly Humbodlt . . . . . . . . . . . . . . . . . . . . . . . . .11,980
Idaho State University . . . . . . . . . . . . . . . . . . . . . .12,037
Northern State University . . . . . . . . . . . . . . . . . . .12,057
Black Hills State University . . . . . . . . . . . . . . . . . .12,206
Montana Tech University . . . . . . . . . . . . . . . . . . . .12,226
Dakota State University . . . . . . . . . . . . . . . . . . . . .12,278
Montana State University . . . . . . . . . . . . . . . . . . .12,312
Utah State University . . . . . . . . . . . . . . . . . . . . . . .12,693
Eastern Washington University . . . . . . . . . . . . . . .12,764
Boise State University . . . . . . . . . . . . . . . . . . . . . . .12,796
University of Idaho . . . . . . . . . . . . . . . . . . . . . . . . .12,914
University of Montana . . . . . . . . . . . . . . . . . . . . . .12,976
South Dakota State University . . . . . . . . . . . . . . . .13,166
University of Alaska Anchorage . . . . . . . . . . . . . . .13,178
Central Washington University . . . . . . . . . . . . . . .13,389
University of Alaska Southeast . . . . . . . . . . . . . . . .13,504
The Evergreen State College . . . . . . . . . . . . . . . . .13,789
University of South Dakota . . . . . . . . . . . . . . . . . .13,809
Western Washington University . . . . . . . . . . . . . .14,204
New Mexico Tech . . . . . . . . . . . . . . . . . . . . . . . . . .14,270
University of Nevada - Reno . . . . . . . . . . . . . . . . .14,468
Fort Lewis College . . . . . . . . . . . . . . . . . . . . . . . . .14,608
University of Utah . . . . . . . . . . . . . . . . . . . . . . . . .15,006

## Annual tuition and fees, from lowest to highest, continued

University of Nevada Las Vegas . . . . . . . . . . . . . . . 15,294
Eastern Oregon University . . . . . . . . . . . . . . . . . . . . 15,390
South Dakota School of Mines . . . . . . . . . . . . . . . 15,600
University of Alaska Fairbanks . . . . . . . . . . . . . . . 15,660
University of Hawaii - Hilo . . . . . . . . . . . . . . . . . . 15,964
Western Oregon University . . . . . . . . . . . . . . . . . . 16,239
North Dakota State University . . . . . . . . . . . . . . . 16,471
Adams State University . . . . . . . . . . . . . . . . . . . . . 16,494
University of Northe Dakota . . . . . . . . . . . . . . . . . 16,541
Colorado Mesa University . . . . . . . . . . . . . . . . . . . 17,240
University of Hawaii - Manoa . . . . . . . . . . . . . . . . 18,162
Portland State University . . . . . . . . . . . . . . . . . . . . 18,471
Southern Oregon University . . . . . . . . . . . . . . . . . 18,644
Western Colorado University . . . . . . . . . . . . . . . . 18,721
Oregon Tech . . . . . . . . . . . . . . . . . . . . . . . . . . . . . . . 18,743
Washington State University . . . . . . . . . . . . . . . . . 18,992
University of Northern Colorado . . . . . . . . . . . . . . 19,122
Arizona State University . . . . . . . . . . . . . . . . . . . . . 19,476
Northern Arizona University . . . . . . . . . . . . . . . . . 19,488
Colorado State University - Pueblo . . . . . . . . . . . . . 20,216
University of Colorado - Colorado Springs . . . . . . 20,478
Metropolitan State University - Denver . . . . . . . . . 22,860
Oregon State University . . . . . . . . . . . . . . . . . . . . . 22,869
Colorado State University. . . . . . . . . . . . . . . . . . . . 24,053
University of Colorado - Denver . . . . . . . . . . . . . . .25,718

## Total approximate cost of attendance

The total approximate cost of attendance includes all costs involved in attending college. This was the most difficult to compare because it varies so much between students. The most common expenses included in the total cost of attendance are books and fees. Books required for classwork can range from a few hundred dollars per year to over a thousand dollars a year. Additional fees above the cost of tuition can range from a few hundred to a few thousand dollars per year. This makes comparing the costs of attendance for WUE schools very difficult. The government requires schools to include these costs in the figures they publish on their websites so students and families have a good idea of the total cost of going to college. However, there is no standard about how to calculate these costs. The types of classes each student takes and what each professor at each school requires their students to purchase for their particular class varies immensely, making comparisons difficult.

As stated earlier, fees are all over the map, which also makes comparisons difficult. Fees can be for technology, activities, the library, maintenance, or whatever the school decides. Some schools may have a few fees that might add up to a couple hundred dollars each year. While others will have fees of over $1,000 for each semester! WUE is 150 percent of in-state tuition (but not fees). Some schools have low tuitions and high fees, while others include almost all costs under tuition. I'm sure there are historical, political or institutional reasons for what is a "fee" and what is "tuition."

The last major factor in the wide range of other costs, especially for WUE students, is the cost of transportation to and from school each year. Some students must fly to go to a WUE school (definitely true in Alaska and Hawaii), while others may drive fifty or a hundred miles. Still others may drive several hundred miles in the fall to bring all their stuff to school, but fly back for winter or spring breaks. How often students return home is also a large cost variable.

The last variable that is hard to compare is just each student's standard of living: cell phone plans, clothing, eating out, entertainment, toiletries, and everyday living expenses are all quite variable, too. Some students spend hardly anything on these expenses, while others spend significantly more. So because these variables make it hard to compare schools, *I've used the same dollar amount ($3,000)* to democratize all these variables. Think of "other costs" as a big pot with fees, books, transportation to and from school, everyday and weekend living expenses all in one expensive dish. So all the school costs will have tuition plus room and board *plus $3,000* to give each WUE student an idea of what the *total* cost of attendance might be. This is different than what is on each school's website, but in a guidebook, I thought this was the best way to compare the schools and give an accurate idea of the costs for WUE students. You'll notice a wide range from under $20,000 to over $30,000 per year. These total costs do not include any aid or scholarships that a student may receive, which would reduce the total costs. Because of possible aid, I wouldn't recommend just eliminating the higher-cost colleges. Think of the total cost of attendance as the most you'll probably pay. Families can refine their actual cost of attendance once they whittle their list down to the schools they're really interested in.

NOTE: The following figures are for the 2019-20 school year. Future rates historically rise 3-5% each year.

**Bottom line: For most students and families, the cost of higher education is a huge factor. Use the WUE tuition, room and board, and total cost of attendance as a known price. Compare it to your in-state colleges and community colleges. Since you often don't know your final tuition costs from either private or public colleges until spring of your senior year, after they've determined how much aid to give you, you can have a good idea of at least these costs and compare them to the final financial-aid offers you receive from all the schools you applied to.**

## Total approximate cost of attendance, from lowest to highest

Utah Tech . . . . . . . . . . . . . . . . . . . . . . . . . . . . . . . . . 21,050
Eastern New Mexico University. . . . . . . . . . . . . . . . 21,910
Southern Utah University. . . . . . . . . . . . . . . . . . . . . 22,105
Montana State University- Northern . . . . . . . . . . . 22,110
Minot State University . . . . . . . . . . . . . . . . . . . . . . . 22,612
Valley City State University . . . . . . . . . . . . . . . . . . . 22,706
Dickinson State University . . . . . . . . . . . . . . . . . . . 22,758
Mayville State University . . . . . . . . . . . . . . . . . . . . . 22,853
Idaho State University . . . . . . . . . . . . . . . . . . . . . . . 23,373
Utah Valley University . . . . . . . . . . . . . . . . . . . . . . . 23,982
University of Montana Western . . . . . . . . . . . . . . . 24,402
Black Hills State University . . . . . . . . . . . . . . . . . . . 24,406
Western New Mexico University . . . . . . . . . . . . . . . 24,760
Weber State University . . . . . . . . . . . . . . . . . . . . . . . 24,921
Montana State University - Billings . . . . . . . . . . . . 24,970
Dakota State University . . . . . . . . . . . . . . . . . . . . . . 26,237
New Mexico Highlands University . . . . . . . . . . . . . 26,356
Nevada State University . . . . . . . . . . . . . . . . . . . . . . 26,972
Northern State University . . . . . . . . . . . . . . . . . . . . 26,979
Utah State University . . . . . . . . . . . . . . . . . . . . . . . . 27,053
New Mexico State University . . . . . . . . . . . . . . . . . 27,423
University of New Mexico . . . . . . . . . . . . . . . . . . . . 27,438
Lewis-Clark State College . . . . . . . . . . . . . . . . . . . . 27,756
South Dakota State University . . . . . . . . . . . . . . . . 27,814
Montana Tech University . . . . . . . . . . . . . . . . . . . . 28,346
University of South Dakota . . . . . . . . . . . . . . . . . . . 28,399
New Mexico Tech . . . . . . . . . . . . . . . . . . . . . . . . . . . 28,620
University of Wyoming . . . . . . . . . . . . . . . . . . . . . . . 28,946
University of Idaho . . . . . . . . . . . . . . . . . . . . . . . . . . 29,050
South Dakota School of Mines . . . . . . . . . . . . . . . . 29,100
Cal Poly Humbodlt . . . . . . . . . . . . . . . . . . . . . . . . . . 30,286
North Dakota State University . . . . . . . . . . . . . . . . 30,849
Montana State University . . . . . . . . . . . . . . . . . . . . 30,892
University of Alaska Southeast . . . . . . . . . . . . . . . . 30,958
Cal Poly Maritime . . . . . . . . . . . . . . . . . . . . . . . . . . . 31,048
University of Hawaii - Hilo . . . . . . . . . . . . . . . . . . . 31,165
University of Montana . . . . . . . . . . . . . . . . . . . . . . . 31,542
Boise State University . . . . . . . . . . . . . . . . . . . . . . . . 31,572
Northern Arizona University . . . . . . . . . . . . . . . . . 31,920
University of Alaska Anchorage . . . . . . . . . . . . . . . 31,922
Eastern Oregon University . . . . . . . . . . . . . . . . . . . . 31,927
Cal Poly Pomona . . . . . . . . . . . . . . . . . . . . . . . . . . . . 32,145
University of Northe Dakota . . . . . . . . . . . . . . . . . . 32,299
Fort Lewis College . . . . . . . . . . . . . . . . . . . . . . . . . . . 32,430

## Total approximate cost of attendance, continued

University of Nevada Las Vegas ..............32,488
Western Oregon University ..................32,767
University of Alaska Fairbanks ..............32,880
Eastern Washington University ...............32,880
University of Nevada - Reno .................33,168
Western Colorado University ................33,804
Central Washington University ..............34,203
Western Washington University ..............34,311
Oregon Tech ................................34,647
Adams State University .....................35,106
Colorado Mesa University ...................35,106
The Evergreen State College ................35,599
University of Utah .........................36,448
Portland State University ..................36,751
Colorado State University - Pueblo .............36,764
University of Hawaii - Manoa ................37,378
University of Colorado - Colorado Springs ......38,978
University of Northern Colorado .............40,186
Arizona State University ...................41,240
Southern Oregon University .................41,507
Washington State University ................41,766
Oregon State University ....................44,074
Metropolitan State University - Denver .........44,518
Colorado State University ..................45,561
University of Colorado - Denver .............46,858

# Acknowledgments

I need to thank some folks who helped make this book possible. First are two of my mentors in the field of educational consulting who gave me the idea to publish this book, Todd Johnson and Dr. Steven Antonoff. Then come my colleagues who graciously contributed their insights from actually visiting these colleges. And most of all, I need to thank the great folks in the various admissions offices and institutional resource offices who helped me by providing and checking my data and answering my questions, all in the name of helping students find the best college for them. Their enthusiasm for helping students was one of the most rewarding parts of this project.

This is a list of the professional contributors who helped give insights from their visits to the various colleges.

Evelyn Jerome-Alexander . . magellancounseling.com
Hailee DeMott . . . . . . . . . . www.demottconsulting.com
Glenda Durano. . . . . . . . . . www.collegeadvisingandplanning.com
Nicole Hoseman . . . . . . . . . onmywayconsulting.com
Erin Mitchell . . . . . . . . . . . . erinmitchell6.wix.com/mcollegeconsulting
Marcia Monma. . . . . . . . . . collegesearchconsultants.com
Jackie Posternick . . . . . . . . . consciouscollgeplanning.com
Sue Zoby . . . . . . . . . . . . . . . missionadmission.sz@gmail.com

Brian Swan, August 2025.

## A note on sources

The major source of the data in this guide is the Common Data Set. I used the 2024-2025 set when available and the 2023-2024 if the college had not published its 2024-2025 set. Some colleges had older sets or I had to get the data directly from the college or other sources. WUE tuition rates, room and board were based on the college's websites for 2025-2026 year.

Below is where the data is located on the common data set:

| | |
|---|---|
| # undergrads | B1 Total degree seeking students |
| % out of state freshmen | F1 |
| % freshmen in housing | F1 |
| % students in housing | F1 |
| Freshman retention | B22 |
| 4-year graduation rate | D/C in B-3 |
| 6-year graduation rate | H |
| ACT/SAT median | C9 |
| Acceptance rate | C1 |

# Alphabetical index

Adams State University . . . . . . . . . . . . . . . . . . . . . . page 60
Arizona State University . . . . . . . . . . . . . . . . . . . . . page 42

Black Hills State University . . . . . . . . . . . . . . . . . . page 164
Boise State University . . . . . . . . . . . . . . . . . . . . . . . page 88

California State Polytechnic Univ. - Humboldt . . page 54
California State Polytechnic Univ. - Maritime . . . page 52
California State Polytechnic Univ. - Pomona . . . . . page 56
California State University, Channel Islands . . . . page 50
California State University, Chico . . . . . . . . . . . . . page 50
California State University, Dominguez Hills . . . . page 50
California State University, East Bay . . . . . . . . . . . page 50
California State University, Northridge . . . . . . . . page 50
California State University, Sacramento . . . . . . . . page 50
California State University, San Bernardino . . . . page 50
California State University, San Marcos . . . . . . . . page 50
California State University, Stanislaus . . . . . . . . . page 50
Central Washington University . . . . . . . . . . . . . . . page 192
Colorado Mesa University . . . . . . . . . . . . . . . . . . . page 62
Colorado State University . . . . . . . . . . . . . . . . . . . page 66
Colorado State University-Pueblo . . . . . . . . . . . . . page 64

Dakota State University . . . . . . . . . . . . . . . . . . . . . page 166
Dickinson State University . . . . . . . . . . . . . . . . . . page 136
Utah Tech . . . . . . . . . . . . . . . . . . . . . . . . . . . . . . . . . page 184

Eastern New Mexico University . . . . . . . . . . . . . . . page 122
Eastern Oregon University . . . . . . . . . . . . . . . . . . . page 150
Eastern Washington University . . . . . . . . . . . . . . page 194
Evergreen State College . . . . . . . . . . . . . . . . . . . . . page 196

Fort Lewis College . . . . . . . . . . . . . . . . . . . . . . . . . page 68

Idaho State University . . . . . . . . . . . . . . . . . . . . . . page 90

Lewis-Clark State College . . . . . . . . . . . . . . . . . . . page 92
Mayville State University . . . . . . . . . . . . . . . . . . . page 138

Metropolitan State University of Denver . . . . . . . page 70
Minot State University . . . . . . . . . . . . . . . . . . . . . page 140
Montana State University. . . . . . . . . . . . . . . . . . . page 102
Montana State University-Billings. . . . . . . . . . . . page 100
Montana State University Northern. . . . . . . . . . page 104
Montana Tech . . . . . . . . . . . . . . . . . . . . . . . . . . . page 106

Nevada State University . . . . . . . . . . . . . . . . . . . page 114
New Mexico Highlands University . . . . . . . . . . . page 124
New Mexico State University. . . . . . . . . . . . . . . page 126
New Mexico Tech. . . . . . . . . . . . . . . . . . . . . . . . page 128
North Dakota State University . . . . . . . . . . . . . page 142
Northern Arizona University. . . . . . . . . . . . . . . . page 44
Northern New Mexico College. . . . . . . . . . . . . . page 249
Northern State University. . . . . . . . . . . . . . . . . . page 168

Oregon State University . . . . . . . . . . . . . . . . . . . page 154
Oregon Tech . . . . . . . . . . . . . . . . . . . . . . . . . . . . page 152

Portland State University . . . . . . . . . . . . . . . . . . page 156

South Dakota School of Mines & Technology . page 170
South Dakota State University. . . . . . . . . . . . . . page 172
Southern Oregon University. . . . . . . . . . . . . . . . page 158
Southern Utah University. . . . . . . . . . . . . . . . . . page 178

University of Alaska Anchorage . . . . . . . . . . . . . page 34
University of Alaska Fairbanks . . . . . . . . . . . . . . page 36
University of Alaska Southeast . . . . . . . . . . . . . . page 38
University of Arizona . . . . . . . . . . . . . . . . . . . . . page 41
University of California, Merced. . . . . . . . . . . . . page 50
University of Colorado at Colorado Springs . . . . page 72
University of Colorado at Denver . . . . . . . . . . . . page 74
University of Hawaii-Hilo. . . . . . . . . . . . . . . . . . . page 82
University of Hawaii-Manoa . . . . . . . . . . . . . . . . page 84
University of Hawaii-Maui . . . . . . . . . . . . . . . . . . page 81
University of Hawaii-West O'ahu . . . . . . . . . . . . page 81
University of Idaho . . . . . . . . . . . . . . . . . . . . . . . page 94
University of Montana . . . . . . . . . . . . . . . . . . . . page 108
University of Montana Western. . . . . . . . . . . . . page 110
University of Nevada-Las Vegas. . . . . . . . . . . . . page 116

University of Nevada-Reno . . . . . . . . . . . . . . . . . . page 118
University of New Mexico . . . . . . . . . . . . . . . . . . page 130
University of North Dakota . . . . . . . . . . . . . . . . . page 144
University of Northern Colorado . . . . . . . . . . . . . page 76
University of South Dakota . . . . . . . . . . . . . . . . . page 174
University of Utah . . . . . . . . . . . . . . . . . . . . . . . . page 180
University of Wyoming . . . . . . . . . . . . . . . . . . . . page 204
Utah State University . . . . . . . . . . . . . . . . . . . . . page 182
Utah Valley University . . . . . . . . . . . . . . . . . . . . page 186

Valley City State University . . . . . . . . . . . . . . . . . page 146

Washington State University . . . . . . . . . . . . . . . . page 198
Washington State University - Tri-Cities . . . . . . . . page 191
Washington State University - Vancouver . . . . . page 191
Weber State University . . . . . . . . . . . . . . . . . . . . page 188
Western New Mexico University . . . . . . . . . . . . . page 132
Western Oregon University . . . . . . . . . . . . . . . . . page 160
Western Colorado University . . . . . . . . . . . . . . . . page 78
Western Washington University . . . . . . . . . . . . . page 200

www.ingramcontent.com/pod-product-compliance
Lightning Source LLC
Chambersburg PA
CBHW071620170426
43195CB00038B/1585